World Myths and Legends

25 Projects You Can Build Yourself

Kathy Ceceri

Illustrated by Shawn Braley

Build It Yourself Series

Nomad Press
A division of Nomad Communications
10 9 8 7 6 5 4 3 2 1
Copyright © 2010 by Nomad Press
All rights reserved.
No part of this book may be reproduced in any form without permission in writing from
the publisher, except by a reviewer who may quote brief passages in a review.
The trademark "Nomad Press" and the Nomad Press logo are trademarks of Nomad Communications, Inc.

This book was manufactured by Sheridan Books,
Ann Arbor, MI USA.
March 2010, Job #314735
ISBN: 978-1-9346704-4-6

Illustrations by Shawn Braley

Questions regarding the ordering of this book should be addressed to
Independent Publishers Group
814 N. Franklin St.
Chicago, IL 60610
www.ipgbook.com

Nomad Press
2456 Christian St.
White River Junction, VT 05001

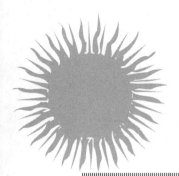

CONTENTS

Timeline ☀ Map

Introduction ~1~

Chapter 1
What Are Myths
and Legends?
~3~

Chapter 2
The Middle East
~14~

Chapter 3
Greece and Rome
~25~

Chapter 4
Northern Europe
~43~

Chapter 5
Sub-Saharan Africa
~56~

Chapter 6
India and China
~64~

Chapter 7
Japan and Australia
~77~

Chapter 8
Central and South
America
~85~

Chapter 9
North America
~98~

Names ☀ Templates ☀ Glossary ☀ Resources ☀ Index

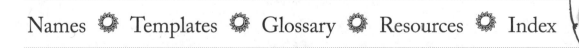

Timeline

BCE

70,000	**Africa**: First ceremonial burials.
65,000	**Australia**: First people arrive.
60,000	**North America**: First people arrive.
50,000	**Japan**: First people arrive.
11,000	**Mesopotamia**: Farming begins.
8500	**Middle East**: Rock drawings of animals appear.
7000	**China**: Farming begins.
5000	**Egypt**: Oldest calendar.
4100	**Africa**: Rice grown in West Africa.
3200	**Egypt**: Hieroglyphics first used.
3000	**Mesopotamia**: Cuneiform writing develops.
3000	**Crete**: Minoan civilization begins.
2650	**Egypt**: Pyramid building begins.
2100	**Mesopotamia**: *Gilgamesh* first recorded.
2000	**China**: Stories of Shang-Ti appear.
2000	**Africa**: Kingdom of Kush founded along southern Nile.
1991	**Egypt**: Book of the Dead collected.
1500–1000	**India**: Hindu *Vedas* composed.
1300	**China**: Writing appears.
1280	**Greece**: Trojan War takes place.
1100	**China**: Shang-Ti replaced by Tian.
1000	**Northern Europe**: Celts emerge.
700	**Greece**: *The Illiad* and *The Odyssey* composed.
500	**Middle East**: Hebrew Bible first written down.
500	**India**: Buddhism founded.
500	**China**: Confucianism and Taoism founded.
500	**Japan**: Rice farming brought from China.
480	**Greece**: Classical Age begins.
400–300	**India**: *Mahabharata* written.
400	**India**: *Ramayana* first collected.
336	**Greece**: Reign of Alexander the Great begins.
200	**Rome**: Conquest of Greece.
110	**China**: Silk Road opens.
52	**Britain**: Romans' first invasion.
30	**Rome**: Virgil writes *The Aeneid*.

TIMELINE

CE

43	**Britain**: Romans conquer Celts.
50	**Middle East**: New Testament of the Bible begun.
65	**China**: Buddhism reaches China.
260	**Japan**: Temple of Amaterasu founded.
300	**Mexico**: Mayan Empire begins.
330	**Rome**: Christianity becomes the official religion.
410	**Britain**: Romans withdraw.
538	**Japan**: Buddhism introduced; Confucianism and Taoism follow.
540	**Africa**: Christianity spreads to Ethiopia.
600	**China**: First books printed.
650	**Middle East**: Koran written.
700	**Ireland**: Celtic myths first written down.
712	**Japan**: *Kojiki* (*Record of Ancient Things*) written.
800	**Scandinavia**: Vikings raids begin.
1000	**Africa**: Islam spread by trade.
1000	**North America**: Iroquois Confederacy formed.
1100	**Scandinavia**: *Poetic Edda* collected.
1150	**Africa**: Yoruba culture at height.
1200	**Scandinavia**: *Prose Edda* collected.
1200	**Peru**: Inca Empire founded.
1275	**China**: Marco Polo visits from Europe.
1300	**North America**: Hopi kachinas appear.
1325	**Mexico**: Aztecs come to power.
1485	**Africa**: Portugese send Christian missionaries.
1492	**North America**: Spanish arrive.
1502	**Africa**: First slaves sent to Americas.
1521	**Mexico**: Spain defeats Aztecs.
1532	**Peru**: Spain defeats Incas.
1606	**Australia**: Europeans arrive.
1946	**Japan**: Emperor Hirohito denies divinity.

BCE stands for Before Common Era. It is a countdown to 0, the year Jesus Christ was born. CE stands for Common Era. It counts up from 0 to the present year.

Important Places

The Americas
1. Mexico
2. Teotihuacan
3. Tenochititlan (present-day Mexico City)
4. Lake Texcoco
5. Guatemala
6. Peru
7. Cuzco (city)
8. Andes Mountains
9. Machu Picchu
10. Lake Titicaca

United States
11. Grafton, New York
12. Flagstaff, Arizona

Europe
13. Mediterranean Sea
14. Greece
15. Athens, Sparta (city-states)
16. Mount Olympus (real mountain)
17. Delphi
18. Ithaca
19. Rome (Italy)
20. Spain
21. Sweden
22. Norway
23. Denmark
24. England
25. Ireland
26. Giant's Causeway (Northern Ireland)
27. Scotland
28. Wales

Important Places

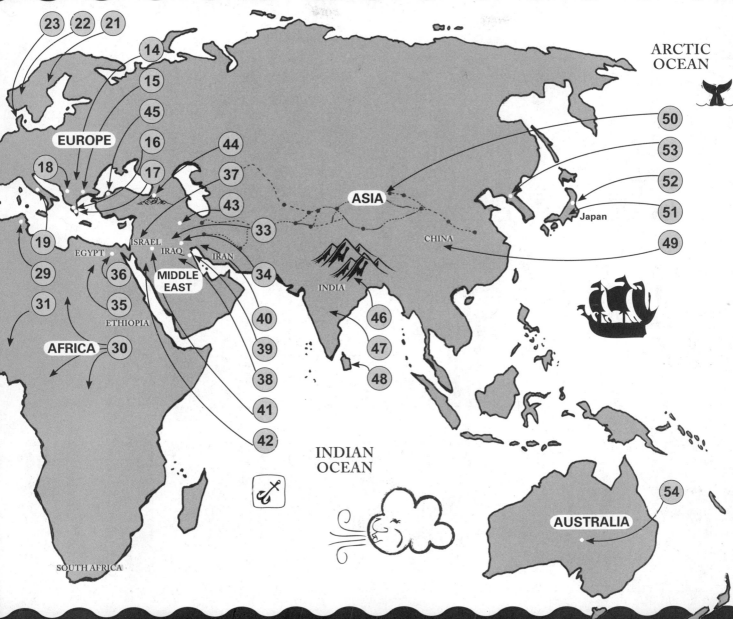

ARCTIC
OCEAN

23 22 21

14

15

45

16

EUROPE

44

18

17

37

43

ASIA

33

50

53

52

51

Japan

49

19

29

EGYPT

ISRAEL

IRAQ

IRAN

CHINA

36

MIDDLE
EAST

34

INDIA

46

31

35

ETHIOPIA

47

AFRICA 30

40

48

39

38

41

42

INDIAN
OCEAN

SOUTH AFRICA

AUSTRALIA

54

Africa

29. Carthage (Tunesia)
30. Sub-Saharan
31. Nigeria and Benin
32. Ghana and the Ivory Coast

Middle East

33. Iraq
34. Tigris and Euphrates Rivers
35. Egypt
36. Nile River
37. Israel
38. Mesopotamia
39. Sumer
40. Uruk (city)
41. Babylon
42. Assyria
43. Nineveh (city)

Asia

44. Mount Ararat (Turkey)
45. Troy (Turkey)
46. Himalaya Mountains (India)
47. India
48. Sri Lanka
49. China
50. Silk Road
51. Japan
52. Mount Fuji
53. Korea

Australia

54. Uluru, or Ayer's Rock

Other titles from Nomad Press

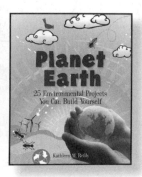

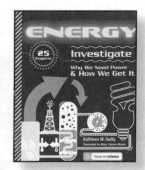

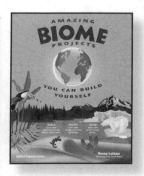

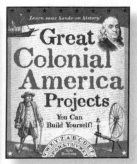

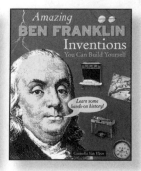

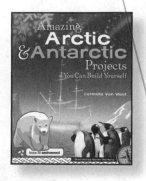

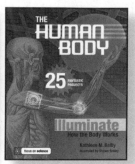

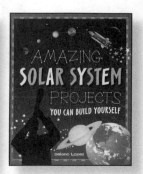

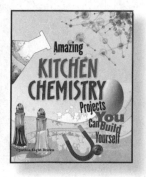

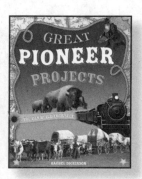

Introduction

Long before there were books or television or movies, people sat around and told each other stories. Some stories made their listeners laugh. Others made them cry or shiver with fear. Some described real-life events of the past or present. And many tried to answer questions that human beings have wondered about since the beginning of time: Why are we here? How does the world work? Why do people act the way they do?

As the stories were told over and over, new storytellers added their own touches. Each version became a little better, until the stories were larger than life. Over generations, the stories once told around an ancient fire came handed down to us as **myths** and **legends**. Today, myths and legends are behind many of the everyday things we take for granted. For instance:

- The month of January is named after Janus, the god of doorways in Roman mythology.
- Thursday is the day of Thor, the Norse god of thunder.
- In *Harry Potter and the Sorcerer's Stone*, Fluffy the three-headed guard dog is based on the Greek story of Cerberus. Cerberus kept watch over Hades, the underworld.
- The Easter Bunny and his basket of eggs are from Eastre, the Anglo-Saxon goddess of spring and rebirth.

World Myths and Legends

Societies all over the world have their own myths and legends. But they are more than just stories. Myths and legends tell us about a people's history, science, and cultural values. They describe what people know, the things they believe in, and what they feel is important.

You'll find that similar themes, characters, and events appear in myths and legends from many parts of the world. This book will help you consider reasons why this happens. With the fun and interesting projects, you can experience the stories yourself.

Words to Know

myth: a story about gods or supernatural creatures that people once believed was true.

legend: a story about national heroes.

culture: the beliefs and way of life of a group of people.

mythologist: someone who studies myths.

god: a superhuman or supernatural being who may have powers.

supernatural or **superhuman:** outside the usual laws of nature, such as magic.

mythology: a collection of related myths from one culture.

religion: a set of beliefs about reality and a god or gods.

literature: the written stories and history of a culture, language, or group of people.

hero: a man, woman, or child who has the strength, wisdom, bravery, or beauty to do tasks that seem impossible.

In this book, you'll hear myths and legends from the Middle East, Europe, Africa, Asia, Australia, and the Americas. Learn about the people who created them, and see how the stories fit into each particular **culture**.

The world of myth and legend is fascinating. It's filled with action and adventure, romance and mystery, battles and betrayals, punishment and rewards. Come enjoy some of the ancient stories people have shared for thousands of years!

Chapter 1
What Are Myths and Legends?

The words myth and legend are sometimes used to describe the same idea: a well-known old story. However, **mythologists** give the terms somewhat different meanings.

⟨✦⟩

A myth is a story about **gods** or magical creatures that people once believed was true. It is part of a **mythology**, a collection of related myths from one culture. A culture's mythology comes from its past or present **religion** or belief system. It can also be the basis of its history, science, or **literature**.

A legend tells the adventures of a **hero** who sets out to do something impossible. A hero may try to save one person or an entire society. Although it may contain supernatural creatures or magic, a legend doesn't usually have gods. Like a myth, it's often considered to be true by the people who first tell it. And in fact it may be based on real people and events. Over time, however, the story grows to become more fantastical than real.

Common Types of Myths

- **Creation Myths** tell how the universe formed. They describe how plants, animals, humans, and gods came into being.
- **Nature Myths** explain how the natural world works, such as why there is day and night and why there are seasons. Some nature myths explain why plants and animals look or behave the way they do.
- **Hero Tales** focus on the adventures of **mortals**. Gods and other supernatural creatures often appear in these stories, too.
- **Trickster Tales** involve **divine** or mortal characters known as **tricksters** who play cruel jokes or try to outsmart those around them. They may be looking for revenge, or just doing it for fun.
- **Death and Afterlife Myths** describe the death of gods or where humans go after they die.
- **End of the World Myths** explore how the universe is destroyed, and what happens afterwards.

Where Myths and Legends Came From

One reason myths and legends developed may be that people needed a way to explain how the world works. In many mythologies, everything in the world is alive or under the control of supernatural beings. These living things often have the same kind of thoughts and emotions people do.

An example is how ancient Egyptians explained day and night. They did not know that day and night are caused by the earth turning in relation to the sun. They explained it with stories about Nut, the goddess of the sky. Nut stretched out above her brother and husband Geb, the earth god. Her feet lay in the east and her head in the west. Shu, the god of air, held up Nut's middle.

Did You Know?

In many mythologies gods are in charge of aspects of the world that reflect their strong personalities. Their special powers make them helpful or dangerous to each other as well as to mortals.

Every day, the sun god Ra would sail up Nut's body in his boat, moving from east to west. At the end of the day, when Ra reached Nut's head in the west, she would swallow him. He would then twinkle inside her body all night long. The next morning, Nut would give birth to him in the east, coloring the sunrise red with the blood of childbirth.

Myths and legends were also used to build group identity. They brought people together under shared beliefs and values. Everyone in a group, nation, or empire would be familiar with the same gods and heroes. Warlike societies had myths about fighting, conflict, and conquest. **Pastoral** societies had myths about plants and animals.

Did You Know?

Fairy tales and folk tales are also traditional stories with magical elements. But they are different from myths and legends because the first people to tell them did not believe they were true.

Some cultures, like the ancient Egyptians, focused on death and what came after death. Their mythology was about how to ensure a good afterlife.

Mythologies could also help keep certain people in power. They did this by making a connection between a society's rulers and its gods. In Japan, for example, people obeyed the emperor because they believed he was descended from the sun goddess Amaterasu. Other myths were used to control people by setting rules and giving warnings. They showed what happened when a human disobeyed the laws laid down by the gods.

Words to Know

mortal: an ordinary human, someone who does not live forever.

divine: to be a god or relating to a god.

trickster: a person, animal, or god who tries to outsmart other characters for fun, greed, or revenge.

pastoral: relating to the countryside or rural life.

rural: in the country, outside the city.

World Myths and Legends

Legends about the bravery and intelligence of heroes inspired people. King Arthur and his Knights of the Round Table were admired for being champions of right over might. Despite their serious purpose, myths and legends were great entertainment. The Greek poet Homer knew this when he composed his two great adventure stories, *The Iliad* and *The Odyssey*.

How Myths and Legends Were Preserved

The earliest myths and legends were part of an **oral tradition**. Most people could not read and write, so cultures passed along important stories by word of mouth. Longer stories were sometimes told as **epic poems** or songs. These used rhyme, rhythm, and repeating phrases and verses to help the storyteller remember what came next. One example is the epic poem Beowulf, which tells about a hero, a monster, and the monster's mother. Written in **Old English**, it's more than 3,000 lines long.

Painting, sculpture, and other visual arts were also used to pass along myths and legends. Many Greek and Roman ruins contain scenes of gods and their stories. Music, dance, and ceremonies were ways to remember myths and legends. Our holiday rituals and customs

Words to Know

oral tradition: a way of passing along important knowledge through spoken storytelling or song instead of writing.

epic poem: a long poem about the adventures of a hero told on a grand scale.

Old English: an early version of English used until about 1150 CE.

archaeologist: a scientist who studies ancient people and their cultures.

hieroglyphic: picture writing from ancient Egypt.

A Sample from Beowulf

Here is one of the opening stanzas of Beowulf, translated from the Old English by Lesslie Hall:

In the boroughs then Beowulf, bairn of the Scyldings,
Belovèd land-prince, for long-lasting season
Was famed mid the folk (his father departed,
The prince from his dwelling), till afterward sprang
Great-minded Healfdene; the Danes in his lifetime
He graciously governed, grim-mooded, agèd.

often come from ancient myths. For example, on Valentine's Day we give out cards and put up decorations with pictures of the Roman god Cupid. Cupid is the baby who flies around shooting arrows of love.

Eventually myths and legends were written down. This allowed people everywhere to read the same version. Authors like Homer and Ovid became famous for their popular retellings of well-known stories. Some of the earliest stories from long-lost civilizations were revived when **archaeologists** discovered these written versions. Many of the Egyptian myths, for example, became known when **hieroglyphics** were found in ancient tombs.

The stories, songs, paintings, and other creations based on myths and legends make up an important part of a society's art and literature. Many of our favorite books and movies today have extra meaning because they are based on much older stories. The filmmaker George Lucas has said his *Star Wars* movies were successful because he studied the work of mythology expert Joseph Campbell.

World Myths and Legends

How Myths and Legends Spread and Changed

Popular myths and legends spread from one country to another through trade, exploration, and warfare. For instance the famous Greek myth of the Minotaur, about a monster that is half-man and half-bull, takes place on the island of Crete. **Scholars** believe the story started there and was later adopted by the Greeks. Archaeologists have found **artifacts** on the island from a bull-worshipping society known as the Minoans. Although no Minoan myths survive, **frescoes** show men and women tumbling over the backs of bulls.

When the Romans conquered the Greeks they adopted the Greek **pantheon**. Although they changed the names of the gods, they kept many of the stories.

At first myths and legends reflect the experiences and values of the culture that created them. But as they travel from one society to another, the details and meanings can change. For instance, Buddhism was founded in India, but later spread to China and Japan. In each place, new Buddhists created their own customs, gods and stories. Also, outsiders who write down stories from the oral tradition of other cultures sometimes change them to fit their own point of view. Some experts believe that this is what happened when **Christian** church officials from Europe recorded **sacred** stories they heard in Africa and the Americas.

Words to Know

scholar: an expert who studies a subject.

artifact: an ancient man-made object.

fresco: a wall painting made in wet plaster.

pantheon: all the gods from one tradition.

Christian: belonging to a religion based on Jesus Christ and the Old and New Testaments of the Bible.

sacred: extremely valuable to a culture, religion, or god.

Ice Age: time when glaciers spread over large parts of the earth, ending around 10,000 years ago.

deity: a god or goddess.

8

What Are Myths and Legends?

Sometimes different cultures have similar myths, even though there is no sign that they ever had contact. How could this happen? One explanation is these stories may have been based on actual events. Take flood myths, in which supernatural rains cause water to cover the Earth. Some scientists believe they date back to the end of the last **Ice Age**. When the glaciers melted, oceans rose around the world. Low-lying areas were flooded. Ancient people near the shore would have seen the water creep up as much as 6 inches (15 centimeters) a day.

Similar stories may have also developed to explain common human experiences. For example, people in many parts of the world must have wondered why plants grow in certain seasons and not others. That may be why there are so many stories about a harvest **deity** who spends part of the year in the underworld.

Did You Know?

A myth or a legend used to be defined as a story that wasn't true. Today, many scholars don't label stories true or false. They prefer to give stories from all traditions the same respect.

Why Some Myths and Legends Faded and Disappeared

Interaction with other cultures is just one way myths and legends changed over time. Sometimes local stories were absorbed into new ones. In Ireland, Brigid, the goddess of fire, became the Christian Saint Brigid, who tended the same fire for hundreds of days.

In other places like the Americas, conquerors replaced local sacred stories with their own. Some societies have even abandoned their own mythology. As their scientific understanding about the world grew, their need for myths disappeared.

Even today, myths and legends have a powerful appeal. They stay popular because they're good stories. But they also live on because they try to answer some of our basic questions in ways that anyone can understand.

Flood Myths Around the World

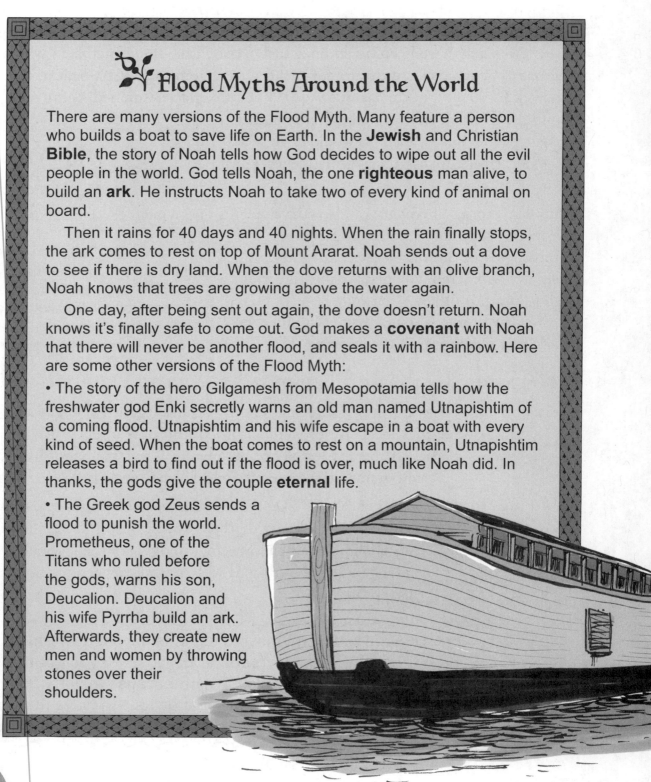

There are many versions of the Flood Myth. Many feature a person who builds a boat to save life on Earth. In the **Jewish** and Christian **Bible**, the story of Noah tells how God decides to wipe out all the evil people in the world. God tells Noah, the one **righteous** man alive, to build an **ark**. He instructs Noah to take two of every kind of animal on board.

Then it rains for 40 days and 40 nights. When the rain finally stops, the ark comes to rest on top of Mount Ararat. Noah sends out a dove to see if there is dry land. When the dove returns with an olive branch, Noah knows that trees are growing above the water again.

One day, after being sent out again, the dove doesn't return. Noah knows it's finally safe to come out. God makes a **covenant** with Noah that there will never be another flood, and seals it with a rainbow. Here are some other versions of the Flood Myth:

• The story of the hero Gilgamesh from Mesopotamia tells how the freshwater god Enki secretly warns an old man named Utnapishtim of a coming flood. Utnapishtim and his wife escape in a boat with every kind of seed. When the boat comes to rest on a mountain, Utnapishtim releases a bird to find out if the flood is over, much like Noah did. In thanks, the gods give the couple **eternal** life.

• The Greek god Zeus sends a flood to punish the world. Prometheus, one of the Titans who ruled before the gods, warns his son, Deucalion. Deucalion and his wife Pyrrha build an ark. Afterwards, they create new men and women by throwing stones over their shoulders.

• In **Hindu** mythology, the world's first man is named Manu. He catches a tiny fish and promises to save it. Manu keeps the fish in a jar, and as it grows he moves it to the Ganges River, then to the ocean. The grateful fish reveals itself to be Brahma, the Creator, and warns Manu of a coming flood. Brahma tells Manu to build an ark so he can protect the seeds of everything on Earth. After Manu's boat comes to rest atop the Himalayan Mountains, he is given a wife, so they can produce the human race.

• The Huichol Indians of Mexico have a story about Watakame, a hard-working farmer, who is warned by Great-Grandmother Earth, Nakawe, that a flood is coming. He fills his boat with corn, beans, fire, and a black dog. The flood lasts five years. After it is over, the dog turns into a woman who becomes Watakame's wife.

Words to Know

Jewish: belonging to the religion based on God in the Old Testament of the Bible.

Bible: holy book shared, in part, by Jewish and Christian people.

righteous: lawful, free from sin.

ark: a boat built by Noah to save his family and animals from the flood.

covenant: a lasting agreement.

eternal: lasting forever.

Hindu: main religion in India.

Make a Rainbow Myth Window hanging

In the Bible, God creates the rainbow as a symbol of his promise never to send another flood to destroy mankind. For the ancient Greeks, the rainbow was the goddess Iris. She carried messages from Earth to the heavens. The **Norse** believed that a rainbow bridge connected Middle Earth with Asgard, the home of the gods. In Japan, the rainbow was considered the Floating Bridge of Heaven. In Australia, the **Aborigines** tell stories about the Rainbow Serpent who creates the rivers and lakes as she moves across the land. And in Africa, Aido-Hwedo is the Rainbow Snake who surrounds the earth, munching on his own tail.

Choose one of these rainbow myths and design your own see-through window hanging based on it. Or come up with your own story to explain what a rainbow is or why it occurs. When you draw with your markers on the clear polystyrene plastic and then heat it, your design will shrink to one-third of its original size and become about nine times thicker.

Supplies

- permanent markers
- recycled polystyrene clear plastic food container (#6 recycle code ONLY!)
- scissors
- hole puncher
- oven or toaster oven (not a microwave oven
- metal baking pan
- aluminum foil
- string

1 With the markers, draw a picture of a rainbow and any other flood myth elements you like on the clear #6 plastic. Be sure to leave space at the top of your design for a hole so that you can hang it from a string.

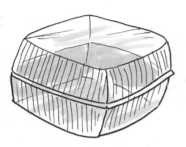

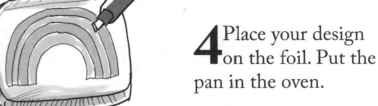

2 Cut out your design. At the top, punch or cut out a hole about ¼ inch from the edge.

3 With an adult's help, heat the oven to 325 degrees Fahrenheit (163 degrees Celsius). Line the baking pan with aluminum foil.

4 Place your design on the foil. Put the pan in the oven.

5 Heat your design for about 2 minutes. It's done after it curls up and flattens out again.

6 Remove the hot pan from the oven carefully. Let your design cool. Then tie the string to the hole at the top, and hang your rainbow where sunlight can hit it.

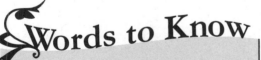

Words to Know

Norse: people from Denmark, Norway, and Sweden.

Aborigine: original people living in Australia.

Chapter 2
The Middle East

The world's oldest civilizations—and its oldest sacred stories and writings—may come from the part of Western Asia and North Africa that includes Iraq, Egypt, and Israel. This area is known as the Middle East.

Thanks to its combination of fertile land, fresh water, and warm climate, people here were some of the earliest farmers. About 13,000 years ago, they learned to grow wheat for flour. Around 9,000 years ago they started raising animals such as goats, sheep, and cattle for meat, milk, wool, leather, and to do work.

The rise of farming meant there was enough food for large cities to grow. And in the cities people began developing other skills. Merchants and craftsmen made clothes, tools, and household goods and sold them in markets. Builders constructed houses and water systems. Engineers designed great **ziggurats** and pyramids. Soldiers joined armies to protect their city and attack others. Artists, entertainers, and religious leaders nurtured people's spirits. And about 5,000 years ago, people in the Middle East began using symbols to keep records and write down the information and stories they wanted to remember and pass on.

ziggurats

The Middle East

Words to Know

ziggurat: ancient Mesopotamian temple shaped like a stepped pyramid with a shrine on top.

cuneiform: wedge-shaped writing.

stylus: a pointed instrument used for writing.

reed: a plant with a straight, tall stalk that grows in or near water.

zodiac: the 12 constellations or "signs" located in the strip of sky that contains the paths of the sun, moon, and planets.

constellation: a group of stars that makes up a picture or shape.

immortality: being able to live forever.

Mesopotamia

Mesopotamia was known as the "cradle of civilization." It occupied the region surrounding the Tigris and Euphrates Rivers in present-day Iraq. The Sumerian, Babylonian, and Assyrian civilizations sprang up here. Along with farming and writing, this region produced some of the earliest examples of monetary and legal systems.

Mesopotamia is where the story of a king named Gilgamesh was first recorded on clay tablets. *Gilgamesh* was written sometime between 2100 and 627 BCE, making it the world's oldest known written epic.

Scholars believe *Gilgamesh* may be based on a real king of Uruk who lived around 2600 BCE.

The epic was first discovered in the 1800s in the ruins of a library in Nineveh, the capital of the Assyrian Empire. *Gilgamesh* was written using a method called **cuneiform**. This early form of writing consisted of marks pressed into a slab of soft clay with the side of a **stylus** made of **reed**. Fragments of the story have since been found in other parts of the Middle East.

Ishtar, the goddess in the story, is the model for other love goddesses such as the Egyptian Isis and the Greek Aphrodite.

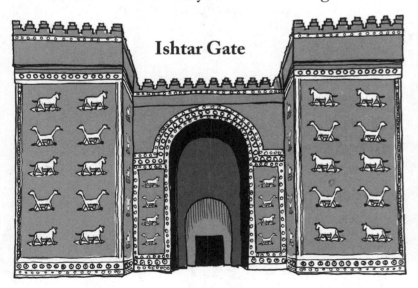

Ishtar Gate

15

Ishtar is also connected with the morning and evening star, which is the planet Venus. The beautiful Ishtar Gate, part of the walls around the city of Babylon, was named after her. Its blue tiles are covered with gold figures of lions, dragons, and bulls. The gate was discovered by archaeologists in 1902, and is now in the Pergamon Museum in Berlin, Germany.

Did You Know?

The 12 signs of the **zodiac** originated in ancient Babylon. For example, the Bull of Heaven in Gilgamesh is now the **constellation** we call Taurus. The goat-fish Enki, who warned Utnapishtim about the coming flood, is the zodiac sign Capricorn.

The Epic of Gilgamesh

Gilgamesh, king of the city of Uruk, is part divine and so energetic his people can't keep up with him. Gilgamesh sets all the men of the city to work on the city walls. Then he chases after all the women. The people of Uruk turn to the gods for help. The gods send Enkidu, a hairy wild man. When Gilgamesh and Enkidu wrestle, the king realizes this wild man is as strong as he is, and they become fast friends. With Enkidu to join their king in adventures, the people of Uruk are relieved.

First Gilgamesh and Enkidu team up to defeat a giant in the woods. Then Gilgamesh rejects the love goddess Ishtar, so she sends the Bull of Heaven to ravish the land. Enkidu helps Gilgamesh destroy the bull, but the gods punish him with a deadly illness. When Enkidu dies, Gilgamesh panics and decides to try to live forever. He seeks out the advice of his ancient relative Utnapishtim, who had won **immortality** for saving mankind from the Mesopotamian flood. Utnapishtim tells Gilgamesh where to find a special underwater plant. If he eats the plant, he will live forever.

Gilgamesh finds the plant. But before he can take a bite, it's snatched away by a snake. The snake gains the ability to renew itself forever by shedding its old skin. And Gilgamesh comes to accept the fact that one day he will die.

Cuneiform Clay Tablet

Students in Mesopotamia practiced writing cuneiform on round clay tablets shaped like flattened balls. These tablets fit neatly in the palm of the hand.

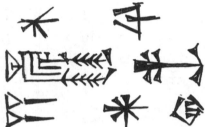

1 Study the cuneiform symbols and decide what you want to write.

2 Flatten out a round piece of clay big enough for your design.

3 To make a cuneiform wedge shape, take the square end of the stick and poke it into the clay so it leaves a triangle-shaped mark. Then bring the edge of the stick down so it makes a "tail" coming out of the triangle.

4 When you're done with your writing, let the clay dry.

Did You Know?

The Sumerian number system was based on groups of 60 as well as groups of 10. (It's why we have 60 minutes in an hour and 360 degrees in a circle.) So the cuneiform symbol for "600" was the symbol for "60" overlapped by the symbol for "10."

Make a Babylonian Zodiac Starfinder

The sun, moon, and planets appear to move through the sky along a path called the **ecliptic**. (In reality, the planets, our moon and the earth are all traveling around the sun on a plane, kind of like a CD spinning around the center.) The Babylonians took the band of stars that form the zodiac and divided it into 12 equal parts, with one constellation for each month. With this star finder, you can tell what zodiac sign is in the sky on any night of the year. It is designed to work in most of the **Northern Hemisphere**.

Supplies

- paper
- pen
- thin cardboard
- glue stick
- scissors
- tape
- brad paper fastener

1 Trace or photocopy the templates for the front (the horizon window) and middle (the star wheel). Larger versions are on pages 110 and 111. Make two copies of the front and use one for the back. If you want, glue the back onto a piece of sturdy cardboard.

2 Cut out all the pieces. Cut out the window on the front only. Tape the front and the back together along the bottom edge.

Words to Know

ecliptic: the path the sun, moon, and planets appear to take across the sky.

Northern Hemisphere: the half of the earth north of the equator.

3 Slip the middle star wheel in between the front horizon window on top and the back piece. The star wheel should stick out the top just enough so that you can see the months and turn the wheel. Tape the sides of the front and back so that the wheel can turn easily.

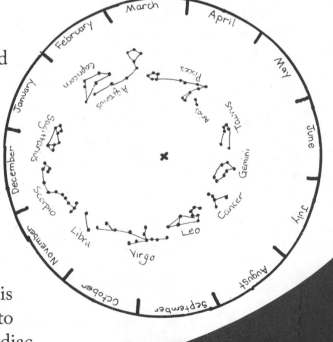

See larger templates on pages 110 and 111.

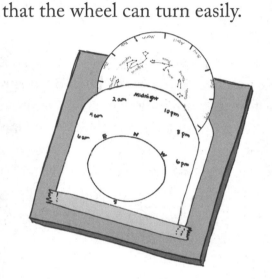

4 Poke the pointy ends of the brad through the "X" on the star wheel and the back. Spread the points so that they hold the pieces together.

5 To use, turn the star wheel until the month and the hour are lined up. Hold the star finder so that the direction you are facing is pointing down. Use the star finder to identify the constellations of the zodiac.

Words to Know

pharaoh: ruler of ancient Egypt.

Sub-Saharan: the part of Africa that lies south of the Sahara Desert.

inundation: a flood.

dynasty: a family that rules a country for a long time.

primeval: from the beginning of time.

chaos: the disorganization before the universe was divided into its separate parts.

embalming: to treat a dead body so it won't decay.

allusion: an indirect reference to something from a story.

Egypt

At the same time civilization was developing in Mesopotamia, Egypt was growing into the first nation in Africa. Egyptians developed their own calendar around 5000 BCE, and started building the famous pyramids in the desert around 2650 BCE. The pyramids were tombs for Egypt's rulers, the **pharaohs**.

Egypt is located along the Nile River, which flows north from **Sub-Saharan** Africa to the Mediterranean Sea. The Nile was the life force of ancient Egypt, providing water for drinking and farming. Its yearly **inundation** covered the fields by the river with mud that fertilized the soil.

Egyptians believed that the royal family was directly descended from the gods.

Pharaohs became gods when they took the throne. New pharaohs were identified with Horus, the falcon-headed sky god. After death, they morphed into Osiris, god of the underworld and judge of the dead. There were hundreds of gods, and different **dynasties** favored different ones. There was no one official Egyptian mythology, so rulers could choose their favorite version.

The Egyptian focus on death is obvious in their lives and in their mythology. Much work and expense went into building elaborate tombs, called pyramids, for their rulers and other important people.

Horus

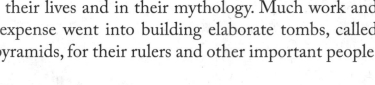

Osiris

An Egyptian Creation Myth

A **primeval** mound rises out of Nun, the ever-flowing source of the Nile's waters. On this hill the gods appear. First comes Ra, the sun god, ruler of the other gods. He creates Shu, the air god, by sneezing. He creates Tefnut, the goddess of moisture, by spitting. Shu and Tefnut become the parents of Geb and Nut, the land and the sky. Geb and Nut then give birth to Osiris, Isis, Seth, and Nephthys. Ra grows old, and passes his rule to Osiris.

Osiris and his sister/wife Isis are the first rulers of Egypt. Osiris teaches mankind useful skills like farming. However, his brother Seth, the god of **chaos**, is jealous of him and wants the throne for himself. He locks Osiris in a box, which he then throws into the Nile. The box floats down to the Mediterranean, where Isis finds it. Osiris is dead, but Isis breathes life into him long enough to conceive a son, Horus.

When Seth discovers that Isis has found the body of Osiris, he cuts the body into pieces and scatters them around Egypt. Isis puts the body back together again with the assistance of Anubis, the god of **embalming**, who has the head of a jackal. Anubis helps Isis prepare Osiris to enter the underworld and become lord of the dead. Seth and Horus ask the other gods to decide who should inherit the throne of Osiris. After long deliberation, the gods decide that Horus should rule Egypt. Seth joins Ra in the sky and becomes god of thunder and storms. And Osiris becomes god of the underworld.

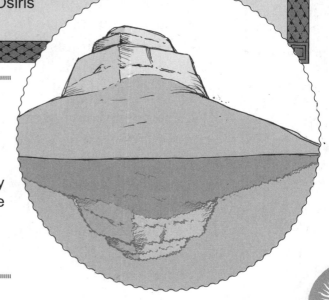

Did You Know?

The story of the primeval mound emerging from the water was probably inspired by the rising and falling of the Nile every year. The pyramids rising above the desert may also be an **allusion** to the mound.

21

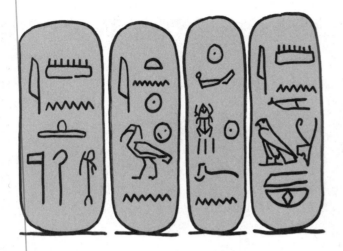

In fact, most of our knowledge about ancient Egypt comes from artifacts placed in the tombs for the use of the departed in the afterlife.

The Egyptians believed that after death they would have to pass many tests to prove their worthiness. At the end of this ordeal, Osiris, the lord of the dead, would weigh their heart against the feather of truth. If their heart was too heavy, the fierce monster Ammut would devour it. If it was light enough, they could dwell in the afterlife with the gods.

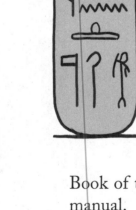

Wealthy Egyptians had tips for passing the tests inscribed on their coffins and on the walls of their tombs. They were also buried with the Book of the Dead, a detailed instruction manual.

Did You Know?

The Book of the Dead and other texts found in ancient Egyptian tombs were written in hieroglyphics. The ancient Egyptians began using this type of picture writing around 3100 BCE. For a long time after hieroglyphics were discovered, no one could **decipher** them. Archaeologists finally got the key they needed in 1799 with the discovery of the Rosetta Stone. It has the same information written in Greek, Demotic (a type of Egyptian script), and hieroglyphics. By comparing words across the three languages, Jean-François Champollion was able to discover the meaning of the hieroglyphics. Today, the Rosetta Stone is in the British Museum in London.

Words to Know

decipher: to figure out the meaning of something.

canopic: a jar used to hold the organs of an ancient Egyptian mummy.

natron: a natural salt used to embalm corpses.

linen: cloth made from fiber of the flax plant.

resin: a sticky fluid made from plants that dries into a hard coating.

amulet: a charm to protect against evil.

Wrap an Egyptian Mummy

The Egyptians invented embalming because they believed a person needed their body to enjoy the afterlife. Mummies last for thousands of years. Ancient Egyptian embalmers first removed the heart and other organs, storing them in separate **canopic** jars, and then dried the body out with a salt called **natron**. The next step was wrapping. The embalmers used up to 4,000 square feet (372 square meters) of **linen** to wrap around the mummy. The wrapping process could take more than a week. It involved soaking the cloth with **resin** and slipping special **amulets** between the layers.

You can try your wrapping technique on a doll or a human volunteer. If you're using a friend, use a new roll of toilet paper. Make sure to leave their nose and mouth uncovered!

Supplies

- markers
- cardboard
- scissors
- doll/action figure or friend
- strips of fabric or bandage gauze (for doll)
- toilet paper (for person)
- tape

1 With the markers, draw some amulet designs, like an ankh, scarab, or Eye of Horus, on the cardboard. Cut these designs out.

2 Wrap the body, head, arms, and legs separately. If you want, make a neat pattern by crossing the strips diagonally. Secure the strips with tape.

3 Wrap the arms and legs together with the body. Place amulets between the layers as you wrap.

4 Wrap a final layer around the entire body, pinning the arms to the sides and the legs together.

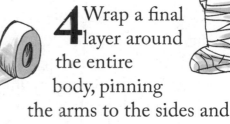

World Myths and Legends

Jewish, Christian, and Islamic Stories

Many of the stories in the **holy** books of the Jewish, Christian, and Islamic religions are similar to myths from other cultures. Even though these religions are **monotheistic**, their stories often contain other supernatural beings like devils and giants or animals that behave in magical ways.

These religions also have their own creation stories. The Bible tells the story of a snake with four legs in the Garden of Eden. The snake tempts Eve, the first woman, into sampling an apple from the Tree of the Knowledge of Good and Evil. But God had forbidden Eve to touch it. God punishes the snake by taking away its legs, so that all snakes must slither in the dirt from that time forward.

Islam's holy book is the **Koran**. It tells how Allah, or God, creates humans from earth, angels from light, and genies from fire. A genie is an invisible **spirit** with special powers. Genies have their own world much like the human world. They also possess the free will to decide whether to be good or evil. The Koran says that King Solomon (the wise king in the Bible) had genie servants, and his wife, the Queen of Sheba, was half genie.

Words to Know

holy: sacred.
monotheistic: the belief in only one god.
Koran: the Muslim sacred book.
spirit: a supernatural being.

Many elements from religious stories appear in today's books and movies.

In the adventure film "Raiders of the Lost Ark," archaeologist Indiana Jones searches for the Ark of the Covenant. This is the magic box that held the Ten Commandments, the laws that God gave Moses in the Bible. *The Lion, the Witch and the Wardrobe*, by C.S. Lewis, retells the story of Jesus using the wise lion Aslan and his magical kingdom of Narnia. Genies have also appeared in stories like *Aladdin*, where they have the ability to grant three wishes to whoever finds them.

Chapter 3
Greece and Rome

When people think of myths, they usually think of the stories of ancient Greece. That's because a series of empires in Europe, Africa, and Asia spread Greek mythology far and wide.

In 336 BCE, the Greek conqueror Alexander the Great captured Egypt and built a famous library there. He even took his armies, and their stories, all the way to the Himalaya Mountains of India. Then around 200 BCE the Roman Empire overthrew the Greeks. They took the Greek gods, gave them new names, and spread their stories further still. In the centuries that followed, other empires, including Britain and Spain, carried Greek influence around the world.

Greek myths are also well known because the Greeks created many lasting works of art celebrating their stories. They produced fantastic sculptures, **mosaics**, pottery, architecture, poetry, and plays. The Romans preserved, copied, and adapted these works, as well as the stories themselves, making them even more famous. Today, artists, architects, and writers still use elements from the **Classical Age** in their work.

Greek and Roman Gods and Goddesses

Many Greek gods and goddesses are still known today, although their Roman names may be more familiar.

Greek Name	Roman Name	Who they are	Usually seen with . . .
Cronus	Saturn	Ruler of the **Titans**, deity of time	**Sickle**, long beard
Zeus	Jupiter	Ruler of the gods	Lightning bolt
Hera	Juno	Queen of the gods	Scepter, tiara, peacock
Poseidon	Neptune	God of the sea	Trident
Hades	Pluto	God of the underworld	Three-headed dog
Aphrodite	Venus	Goddess of love	Floating sea shell
Apollo	Apollo	God of light, music, and medicine	**Lyre**, laurel wreath
Artemis	Diana	Goddess of the hunt	Bow and arrow
Ares	Mars	God of war	Spear
Athena	Minerva	Goddess of wisdom	Owl
Hermes	Mercury	God of merchants and thieves	**Caduceus**, winged sandals, and helmet
Hephaestus	Vulcan	God of fire	Axe
Nike	Victoria	Goddess of victory	Huge wings, no head
Eros	Cupid	God of desire	Diaper, wings, and arrows
Dionysos	Bacchus	God of wine	Grapes and big belly
Pan	Faunus	God of woods and fields	Goat legs
Hestia	Vesta	Goddess of the **hearth**	Fire in the hearth
Demeter	Ceres	Goddess of the harvest	Bundle of wheat

Words to Know

mosaic: a picture or design made from tiny tiles or stones.

Classical Age: the period of great accomplishments in the Greek and Roman Empires.

Titans: in Greek mythology, a race of giant deities who rule the earth before the gods.

sickle: a cutting tool with a curved blade.

lyre: a type of small harp.

caduceus: a rod with two snakes twisted around it.

hearth: fireplace for cooking in the home.

Did You Know?

Prometheus, whose name means "forethought," had a brother named Epimetheus, or "afterthought." Epimetheus' wife was the famous Pandora, or "all gifts." She was the first woman, a present from the gods to mankind. Pandora came equipped with a jar that she was not supposed to open. But she was curious, so she opened it anyway. Out popped all the evils of the world—Sickness, Despair, and War. Quickly she closed the lid, catching Hope inside before it could leave. Today a "Pandora's Box" is a bunch of trouble that's better kept under wraps.

Mythic Allusions Collage

An allusion is an indirect reference to something else you may know. Take some old magazines and look through the illustrations. Is there an ad for Nike shoes? A picture for Valentine's Day featuring baby Cupid? Or a drawing of Old Father Time (Cronus) ringing in the New Year?

Supplies

- magazines
- scissors
- posterboard
- gluestick

See how many images you can find that are allusions to Greek and Roman myths. Then cut them out and make a classical mythology collage. Your collage, a picture created from different images that have been cut out and re-arranged, can show how ancient myths are present in modern life.

Greek Mythology

Ancient Greece was made up of separate city-states like Athens and Sparta. They were basically mini-countries with their own rulers and values. Much of the countryside was too rocky and mountainous for farming. But with miles of jagged coastline along the Mediterranean Sea and countless islands, the Greeks were superb at fishing and sailing. As they sailed around, they came into contact with other cultures. This led to them borrowing from the mythologies of places like Egypt, Mesopotamia, and Crete.

Did You Know?

Zeus and his wife Hera rarely get along in Greek myths. Some scholars believe they fight because Hera represents an older goddess from an earlier culture who was once powerful. The bickering represents the conflict between old and new mythologies.

Mycenae is another early civilization that influenced Greek development. It is believed to have been the country that fought Troy in the Trojan War.

At its height, Athens became the center of Greek art, architecture, literature, and science. In time, belief in the old myths decreased. They came to be seen as cultural symbols, rather than explanations of how the world worked.

The layering of one set of stories upon another may explain why the Greek creation myth—like those in other societies—features one group of powerful beings taking over from another. This version is taken from the **Theogony** by Hesiod, a poet who lived around 700 BCE.

Words to Know

theogony: an account of the beginnings and family connections of the gods.

furies: female monsters with leathery wings who seek revenge on mortals.

Clash of the Titans—and the Gods

First comes chaos. Then from the chaos comes Gaea, or Mother Earth. Gaea gives birth to the sky, Uranus, as well as the mountains and the sea. She mates with Uranus, and gives birth to the powerful Titans. But she also produces monsters with 100 hands and 50 heads, and the one-eyed Cyclopes. Uranus hates these horrible children. So instead of letting them be born from their Mother Earth, he keeps them trapped in a cave. Gaea gives the youngest Titan, Cronus, a sickle to free his brothers and sisters. Cronus uses it to cut down the old ruler. Giants, the **Furies**, and other monsters spring up from the blood that drips from wounds Cronus gave to Uranus. And what flows into the sea creates Aphrodite, the goddess of love.

Cronus becomes ruler, and goes on to create more Titans and other deities. He and his sister/wife Rhea also produce six gods. But Cronus—afraid of suffering the same fate as his father—swallows each child as it is born. Finally, Rhea manages to smuggle out her last baby, named Zeus, by tricking Cronus into swallowing a rock wrapped in a blanket.

Zeus grows up on Earth. When he is old enough, he asks the Titans and the Cyclopes to help him challenge Cronus. First, he slips his father a potion to make him throw up the other gods (and the stone). Then they battle Cronus, and win. Gaea asks her children to make Zeus their leader, but civil war breaks out instead. In the end, the Titans are defeated, and Zeus becomes king. He takes the other gods and goddesses to Mount Olympus. From there, they watch the doings of men on Earth.

Words to Know

rational thinking: thinking based on facts or reasons more than opinion or emotion.

patron: supporter.

origin myth: creation myth.

forge: a furnace for melting metal to make tools and other objects.

Greek Ideals

Greek myths are full of passion and conflict. Especially in Athens, though, the Greek ideals were intelligence, wisdom, logic, and **rational thinking**. Athena, the goddess of wisdom, was the city's **patron**. Her temple, the Parthenon, was built on the Acropolis, a hill overlooking Athens. It's one of the most important and impressive examples of Greek architecture still standing.

In her **origin myth**, Athena springs from Zeus' brow fully grown. Zeus had asked Hephaestus, the god of the **forge**, to split his head open to cure a pounding headache. It turns out Zeus had transformed Athena's mother, Metis, into a fly and swallowed her. The clever Metis had been hammering away, making her daughter-to-be a set of armor. Athena became the goddess of warfare and strategy.

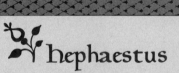

Hephaestus

Hephaestus was the choice to crack Zeus' head open because he was handy with a hammer. He was born to Hera, who tossed him out of Olympus because of his ugly face and deformed legs. On Earth, he learned to forge beautiful things from metal. He used this skill to trick his mother into letting him back to Olympus. He made her a golden throne, but when she sat on it, the throne held her captive. She not only let Hephaestus return, she also gave him the lovely Aphrodite as a wife. Hephaestus was generally kind and even-tempered. But when the Romans turned him into Vulcan, he added "god of volcanoes" to his resume.

⟡ Words to Know

Hydra: a many-headed monster.

Amazon: a race of female warriors.

democracy: a government where the people are represented.

lever: a rod used for lifting things.

catapult: an ancient military machine for hurling objects.

steam engine: a machine powered by boiling water.

Did You Know?

Heracles, known to Romans as Hercules, was half god, half mortal. He's best known for his Twelve Labors. These were tasks he agreed to undertake because of guilt over unknowingly killing his family. His Labors included fighting the **Hydra** and fighting Cerberus, and stealing the belt of the **Amazon** queen Hippolyte. When he cleaned out the Augean Stables, which were filled with cow dung, he used a river, not a broom. In the end, he was rewarded with a home in Olympus.

She's sometimes equated with Nike, the goddess of victory in both battle and sports.

Athena was also the goddess of skilled crafts, such as ship-building and chariot-building. She's said to have invented the potter's wheel and vases. And she was a skilled weaver—but not as good as the mortal Arachne. Arachne challenged Athena to a spinning contest, and won. In most stories the goddess was cool-headed. But in this myth she lost her temper—and turned Arachne into a spider. That's why spiders are also called arachnids.

Greek Inventions

The Greeks were big on inventions. They came up with **democracy,** the notion that all citizens have the right to a voice in government. They also developed a lot of the basics of science and math that we use today. Euclid and Pythagoras made rules about geometry that are still taught in school. The mathematician Archimedes described the working of **levers**, a type of simple machine. Even the **catapult** and the **steam engine** were first invented in ancient Greece.

Greek mythology also celebrated immortals and humans who helped people figure out the world. Prometheus, a Titan who sided with Zeus in the standoff with the gods, created mankind. To help his creation survive, he stole some fire, which made Zeus angry. Zeus had him chained to a rock, where an eagle ate his liver every day, over and over. He was eventually rescued by the hero Heracles.

Did You Know?

Mount Olympus, the home of the gods in Greek mythology, is an actual mountain in Greece.

One of the most clever characters in Greek mythology was Daedalus, an inventor and craftsman from Athens.

In one story Daedalus had a nephew who invented the saw after noticing the sharp backbone of a fish, and also came up with a drawing tool called a **compass**. Daedalus grew so jealous he pushed his nephew off a cliff. Athena rescued the boy and turned him into a partridge. But Daedalus was banished. He went with his son Icarus to Crete, where King Minos needed a **labyrinth** to imprison the half-bull, half-man Minotaur.

Every nine years, Athens had to send a group of youths to Crete to be **sacrificed** to the Minotaur. But one year Theseus, the son of the king of Athens, went along to try to kill the monster. Ariadne, the daughter of King Minos, fell in love with Theseus. She asked Daedalus for help. He told Ariadne to give Theseus a ball of string to unwind as he walked through the labyrinth, so he could follow it back out when the Minotaur was dead. Theseus was successful, but left Ariadne behind when he returned home.

Words to Know

compass: a tool for drawing circles that has two arms joined at the top by a hinge, which can open and close.

labyrinth: a maze.

sacrifice: killing a person or other living thing as an offering to a god or supernatural creature.

shrine: a special place of worship.

panacea: something that is supposed to cure everything.

Greece and Rome

King Minos locked Daedalus and Icarus in a high tower as punishment. To escape, Daedalus and Icarus made themselves wings out of wax and bird feathers. They put them on, jumped from the window, and glided away. Their plan was working perfectly, until Icarus tried some fancy flying. He went too close to the sun. The sun's warmth melted the wax, and the foolish Icarus tumbled into the sea.

The Arts and Sciences

Arts and sciences of all kinds were prized by the Greeks. Apollo, who was skilled in many of them, was one of the most popular gods. He was the god of healing and the father of Asclepius, god of medicine. The Romans built **shrines** to Asclepius, complete with relaxing mineral baths.

Asclepius' daughter Hygeia, the goddess of health, had a pet snake that liked to wrap itself around her father's rod. Today a stick with a snake twisted around it is a symbol of medicine.

Did You Know?

Apollo's areas of interest also included archery, poetry, painting, and music. In one story, the god Hermes, who was only two days old, stole some of Apollo's cattle. When Apollo tracked them down, Hermes showed him a lyre he made from the cow gut and a turtle shell. He also showed him how to make pipes out of reeds. After that Apollo forgave Hermes, and he and the new god became friends.

Doctors today take the Hippocratic Oath in the name of Apollo, Asclepius, Hygeia, and **Panacea**, the goddess of healing potions.

Hippocrates was a Greek physician who taught his students to treat the whole person and not just the symptoms. He also advised patients to live a healthy life to help the body fight disease on its own.

Fortune-Telling Fumes at Delphi

Apollo was also the god of **prophecy**. One of the most famous temples to Apollo was the one located at Delphi. It was built over a **fissure** in the earth, which reportedly gave off sweet-smelling fumes. When people came to the temple seeking advice, the **oracle**, called the Pythia, who was supposed to be able to tell the future, would sit over the fissure and breathe in the fumes. Eventually, she would go into a trance and start to speak. The other priests and priestesses at the temple would explain the hidden meaning in her words.

For centuries, scientists tried to discover the secret of the fumes. In 2000, they found a gas called ethylene seeping from the fissure. In the past, ethylene has been used to put patients to sleep during operations. Scientists believe that, since the time of the oracle, small earthquakes have closed up the fissure. As a result, only tiny amounts of ethylene fumes come wafting up from below today.

Words to Know

prophecy: being able to tell the future.

fissure: crack in the ground.

oracle: someone who makes mysterious prophecies

equilateral triangle: a triangle with three equal sides.

arc: part of a circle.

Make a Triangle with a Compass and Ruler

Supplies

- paper
- pencil
- straight edge, such as a ruler
- math compass with pencil

The Greek mathematician Euclid came up with rules for drawing different geometric shapes using only a compass and a straight edge. In this activity, you'll learn how to make an **equilateral triangle**.

1 Make the base of your triangle by holding the pencil up against the straight edge and moving the point along until you have a straight line.

2 Take the compass and put the point on one end of the line. Open it up so it is as wide as you would like the sides of your triangle to be. Using the pencil end of the compass, draw an **arc** that crosses the line and goes up past where you think the top of your triangle will be.

3 Without changing the opening of the compass, move the point to the place where the arc crosses the line. Draw another arc that crosses the first arc and the straight line.

4 Use the straight edge to connect the places where the lines cross to create your triangle.

The Trojan War and Three Great Epics

The Trojan War connects Greek and Roman history. That is, history in the form of myths as put down in three great epics. Around 700 BCE, the Greek poet Homer composed *The Iliad* and *The Odyssey*. *The Iliad* described how the Trojan War began because of a beautiful woman, Helen of Troy. The Greeks fought Troy for 10 years to bring her back again.

Did You Know?

The name *Iliad* comes from Ilium, another name for Troy.

Helen of Troy

But when the Greek army set sail for home, it was not the end of their adventures. During their **siege** of Troy, the Greeks had offended several gods. In return, these angry gods—among them Poseidon, god of the sea—scattered the Greek fleet of ships across the Mediterranean Sea. *The Odyssey* is about what happened to Odysseus (Ulysses, to the Romans) and his men on the way home to Ithaca. The journey took another 10 years and carried them to many lands inhabited by supernatural creatures. An **odyssey** has come to mean a wandering adventure.

The Real-Life Troy

For generations scholars wondered whether the story of the Trojan War was true. Then in the 1870s amateur archaeologist Heinrich Schliemann discovered the real-life Troy in Turkey, across the Mediterranean Sea from Greece. Several different cities once existed on the same spot, each built upon the ruins of the one before. Scientists today believe the city of *The Iliad* was destroyed in a battle around 1180 BCE. Among the clues they found were piles of bullets for **slings**. If the early Trojans had won that battle, researchers think, they would have picked up their bullets and taken them home to use another day.

Homer's stories have been an inspiration to many other writers through the ages. One of the first was the Roman poet Virgil. In 30 BCE, Virgil picked up where *The Iliad* and *The Odyssey* left off. In *The Aeniad*, he followed the Trojans as they left their city in defeat and set out to found Rome.

The Story of *The Iliad*

When Peleus marries the sea nymph Thetis, the goddess Eris is not invited. Eris decides to make trouble. She sends a golden apple to the feast marked "For the Fairest." Immediately three goddesses—Athena, Hera, and Aphrodite—all claim the prize. Zeus asks Paris, the son of King Priam and Queen Hecuba of Troy, to judge a beauty contest between the goddesses.

Did You Know?

The phrase "the face that launched a thousand ships," referring to Helen, and the saying "beware of Greeks bearing gifts" both come from the story of the Trojan War.

Words to Know

siege: blocking off a city with an army to force it to surrender.
odyssey: a wandering adventure.
sling: a weapon made with a strap for throwing small objects.
vulnerable: unprotected.

Achilles, son of Thetis, goes on to become Greece's finest warrior

Each tries to bribe Paris. Athena promises him wisdom and Hera promises him power, but Paris picks Aphrodite, who promises him the most beautiful woman in the world. She helps him steal Helen, a daughter of Zeus. But Helen is already married to King Menelaus of Sparta. Menelaus gathers the other Greek princes and sets sail for Troy. War breaks out, with the gods and goddesses taking sides.

For ten years the Greeks camp outside the city walls, and the Trojans lie trapped inside. Hector, King Priam's oldest son, kills the Greek hero Patroclus, Achilles' best friend. Achilles takes his revenge by killing Hector and leaving his body to rot. This angers the gods. Cowardly Paris manages to kill Achilles by shooting him in the heel— his one **vulnerable** spot—with a poisoned arrow.

City of Troy

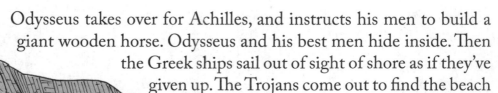

World Myths and Legends

Odysseus takes over for Achilles, and instructs his men to build a giant wooden horse. Odysseus and his best men hide inside. Then the Greek ships sail out of sight of shore as if they've given up. The Trojans come out to find the beach deserted except for the horse. Thinking it must be a gift, they wheel it into the city. At night Odysseus and his men come out and open the gates, letting the rest of the Greek troops inside. Troy is destroyed and the war is won.

The Story of *The Odyssey*

Odysseus and his ships get blown off course to the island of the Cyclopes, one-eyed giants who live in caves. The crew ends up trapped in the cave of Polyphemus, a sheep herder. The giant eats four of Odysseus' men before Odysseus comes up with a plan. They blind the monster with a hot wooden stake. Then, when Polyphemus lets his sheep out in the morning, Odysseus and his remaining men escape by clinging to the animals' bellies.

When they set sail again, a mishap with a bag of wind destroys all but one of Odysseus' ships. And when they stop at the island of the witch Circe, she turns all of the men into pigs. Odysseus convinces Circe to restore them, and they spend a year feasting and carrying on. But Odysseus realizes it's time to move on.

Next the crew pays a visit to the underworld, where Odysseus chats with the shades of his former comrades, including Achilles. Then they sail past the sirens—monsters whose beautiful singing lures sailors into the rocks. Odysseus has his men stop up their ears so they won't be tempted to crash the ship. But he has them tie him to the mast so he can hear the beautiful singing without danger.

Achilles' heel

An **Achilles' heel** is a person's weak spot. According to one myth, Achilles' mother Thetis dunked her baby in the River Styx—which marks the boundary between this world and the next—to give him immortality. But she held him by his ankle, which didn't get the magic treatment. Everyone has an Achilles tendon—a cord running up the back of the leg that connects the heel to the calf muscle. If it's injured, which happens a lot in sports, it's hard to walk, run, or jump.

Words to Know

Achilles' heel: a person's weak spot.

siren song: a call that tempts you to your doom.

strait: a narrow passageway in a body of water.

whirlpool: a spinning funnel of water that can pull things down.

After making it safely past the sea monsters Scylla and Charybdis, Odysseus and his crew reach the island of Helios the sun god. But when the starving men eat the forbidden Cattle of the Sun, Helios destroys them. Only Odysseus is left to wash up on the island of another enchantress, Calypso. He stays with her for eight years before Athena frees him. Then he escapes on a raft and is picked up by some helpful Phaeacians, who send him home to Ithaca in a magic ship.

Once home, there is one more obstacle to face. Odysseus' palace is filled with suitors who want to marry his wife Penelope and take his place as king. But she's as resourceful as her husband. Penelope tells the suitors she won't remarry until she finishes weaving—then secretly unravels her work each night. Odysseus disguises himself as a beggar, and with the help of his son Telemachus and Athena, he drives off the suitors and reunites with his family at last.

Did You Know?

Today's version of the **siren song** might be commercials that make you want things you don't really need.

Make an Odyssey Whirlpool

Scylla and Charybdis were sea nymphs-turned-monsters who guarded a narrow **strait** in the Mediterranean. Scylla was transformed by a jealous Circe into a beast that hid among dangerous rocks, grabbing passing sailors with her six snakelike heads. Zeus punished Charybdis, Poseidon's daughter, for flooding the land during storms. He turned her into a giant mouth, a **whirlpool** who swallowed ships whole. Odysseus was advised to steer closer to Scylla, who at most would eat six of his crew, because Charybdis could destroy his whole ship.

Whirlpools are caused by currents, winds and tides. They're often strongest in shallow straits. To see the power of a whirlpool, try adding food coloring to the water when you make this model.

Supplies

- two 2-liter clear plastic soda bottles (empty and clean)
- water
- food coloring (optional)
- scissors
- duct tape

1 Fill one bottle two-thirds full of water. If you want, add a drop of food coloring.

2 Cover the opening of each bottle with a strip of tape.

3 Take the scissors and poke a hole in each piece of tape a little smaller than the opening of the bottle.

4 Turn the empty bottle upside down and place it on top of the first bottle. Tape the bottles together. Use enough tape to make them secure and leak-proof.

5 To use, turn the whirlpool maker so the bottle with water is on top. Hold the bottom bottle in one spot and swirl the top bottle around. The swishing water will soon form a whirlpool.

Roman Mythology

After defeating Greece, the Romans combined the Greek myths with their own sacred traditions. Why? Because the Greek myths were much more lively and entertaining. Before their contact with the Greeks, the Romans had not thought of the gods as individuals with distinct personalities and complicated social lives. Instead, they had just viewed them as spirits, serving as protectors of everything from war to door hinges.

Did You Know?

When Aeneas leaves Dido to continue his journey to Italy, she curses him and promises eternal hatred between her city and his. In 218 BCE, Rome used this curse as a reason to attack Carthage and its ruler Hannibal.

The Roman gods joined the new Greek gods in the Roman pantheon. For example, Janus, the god of doorways and new beginnings, was the founding Roman god. Images of Janus have two faces, one looking ahead, and one looking behind. The first month of the year, January, is named after him.

The Romans created their own myths when necessary. In order to give Emperor Augustus Caesar a claim to divine origins, the poet Virgil created *The Aeneid*. Virgil transformed a minor Trojan character from *The Iliad*, named Aeneas, into the hero of his story. In *The Aeneid*, Aeneas is the son of a mortal man and the goddess Aphrodite, and a prophecy says that he will father a line of Roman rulers.

The Great Mother

In 204 BCE, a statue of the ancient goddess Cybele, the Great Mother, was brought to Rome from Turkey. Cybele quickly became a popular mythic figure in Rome. Her followers held celebrations every spring called hilaria. These events were so wild that the Roman government ended up banning them. They may be the origin of both April Fool's Day and the English word "hilarious."

The Founding of Rome from *The Aeneid*

What happens to the Trojans after they are defeated at the end of the Trojan War? In this story, Aeneas flees the city and sets out with his men for Italy. On the way, they stop in Carthage, and he falls in love with Dido, the city's queen. For a while, he considers remaining in Carthage. He could marry Dido and become king. But the gods remind him that his destiny is to found a new Troy in Italy. So he leaves Dido, who kills herself in sorrow. Continuing on to Italy, Aeneas fights for the right to wed Livinia. She is the daughter of King Latinus, who rules the Latin people of Italy. With the help of Venus, he wins the battle and claims Livinia. Their marriage unites the Trojan and Latin people.

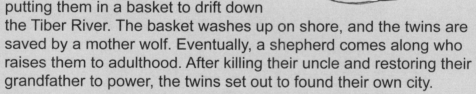

For generations, Aeneas' descendants rule the kingdom. The brother of one of these kings is envious, and overthrows him. The brother forces the king's daughter, Rhea Silvia, to become a Vestal Virgin. He does not want her to have children who could seek revenge on him. But Rhea has the twins Romulus and Remus, with the war god Mars. Right after they are born, her uncle tries to kill them by putting them in a basket to drift down the Tiber River. The basket washes up on shore, and the twins are saved by a mother wolf. Eventually, a shepherd comes along who raises them to adulthood. After killing their uncle and restoring their grandfather to power, the twins set out to found their own city.

In honor of the mother wolf who saved them, Romulus and Remus decide to build their city at the spot along the Tiber River where she found them. But they argue over exactly where it is. In anger, Romulus kills Remus. He then builds the city and names it Rome, after himself.

Chapter 4
Northern Europe

In parts of Europe outside the Roman Empire, a people we call the Celts had their own mythology. In many places, their culture didn't survive as the Roman Empire expanded northward and invaded their lands. Only at the very edges of Roman territory, in Ireland, did entire bodies of stories last long enough to be collected in writing.

After the Romans left, new invaders moved in. Vikings from the Scandinavian countries of Sweden, Norway, and Denmark spread out into Northern Europe and the British Isles. They brought with them a whole new pantheon of Norse gods. Like the Greek and Roman deities, some of these have made their way into modern popular culture. So have bits and pieces of Celtic sacred traditions. And England has also produced some long-lasting heroes of legend, including Beowulf and King Arthur.

Celtic Mythology

From 1000 BCE until they were conquered by the Romans in 43 CE, the Celts controlled much of northern Europe. We know the Celts were talented metalworkers, but they didn't leave behind writings, temples, or monuments to their deities. For this reason little is known about Celtic gods.

The Romans found the Celts to be fierce warriors. They would storm into battle naked and painted blue, with bagpipes wailing in the background. The Celtic priests, called **druids**, were so powerful that the Roman invaders had them destroyed.

Since the druids were the ones who passed down their stories and traditions, that knowledge was destroyed, too.

Did You Know?

The tradition of throwing a coin in a wishing well probably comes from the Celtic custom of offering objects to bodies of water.

The most complete Celtic stories we have today are the Lebor Gabála Érenn, or "Book of Conquests." They were recorded by Christian priests many centuries after Celtic mythology had started to die out.

Words to Know

druid: ancient Celtic priest.
leprechaun: a little magical person from Irish mythology.
causeway: a raised path across water.

The Lebor Gabála Érenn tells how Ireland was settled by five divine races. The fifth race was the Tuatha Dé Danann. They were created by Danu, goddess of the wind, wisdom, and fertility and led by Dagda, god of life and death, war, banquets, and magic.

Danu's grandson Lugh, the god of light, was one of their greatest champions. His son Cuchulainn is the hero of many Irish folktales. But as Celtic stories lost their popularity, Lugh was downgraded from god to magical being. Today Lugh's image survives in stories of Irish **leprechauns**.

Another popular Celtic hero is Finn MacCool. One story explains how he built the Giant's Causeway, a geological formation along the coast of Northern Ireland.

Did You Know?

Some Celtic holidays are still celebrated today. Beltane honors Belenus, god of farming, on May 1. It has become May Day, a spring festival celebrated in many places with maypoles and bonfires. Samhain, the end of the harvest on October 31, is also a time when spirits enter our world. It's why we dress up like ghouls and go trick or treating on Halloween.

Finn MacCool and the Giants Causeway

Finn MacCool is a giant who lives in Ireland, across the sea from another giant named Benandonner, who lives in Scotland. Finn challenges Benandonner to a test of strength. He builds a **causeway** so his rival can cross the sea to Ireland. But after the causeway is built Finn is so exhausted he falls asleep.

The next morning, Finn's giant wife Oonagh wakes up to find Benandonner has arrived and is ready for his fight. Oonagh quickly realizes that Benandonner is much larger than her husband, and comes up with a way to save him. She dresses the sleeping Finn in baby clothes. When Benandonner demands to know where Finn is, Oonagh tells him to be quiet or he'll wake the baby. Benandonner takes one look at the giant "baby" and decides he'd rather not fight the father. Benandonner dashes back across the causeway, destroying it as he runs.

The Giant's Causeway is a tightly packed group of 40,000 tall stone columns jutting out into the sea. The columns are mostly **hexagonal**, about as big around as a stepping stone. The sides of the columns are so straight that they look like they were cut by hand. But they were really formed when **molten** volcanic basalt rock flowed up through fissures in the ground and cracked as it cooled.

King Arthur and the Knights of the Round Table

The legend of King Arthur that most of us know today is set in the **Middle Ages**. It's based on an epic poem by Thomas Malory called *Morte d'Arthur*, or "death of Arthur." In this version, Arthur and his Knights of the Round Table lived in the castle at Camelot. They wore suits of armor and carried long sharp **lances**, which they used to compete at **jousts** and to kill dragons.

But the legendary Arthur may be based on a real military commander who defended Britain against invaders around 500 CE. And the Arthur stories may be even older, going back to myths the Irish brought with them to Wales.

Words to Know

hexagonal: having a shape with six straight, equal sides.

molten: melted.

Middle Ages: a period of time in Europe from the 400s to the 1400s CE.

lance: a sharp spear used by knights on horseback.

joust: a competition using weapons on horseback.

tournament: a series of knightly jousts and other competitions.

anvil: a heavy iron block used with a hammer for shaping metal.

page: a boy working as a knight's assistant.

According to legend, Arthur was a king who tried to unite England. His wise advisor, the magician Merlin, was probably a holdover from the ancient druids. Arthur designed his Round Table so that there would be no "head of the table." He wanted all the knights to feel equal.

The Sword in the Stone

When King Uther Pendragon dies, all the knights are called to London for a **tournament** to decide who should become the next king of England. The magician Merlin has stuck a sword into an **anvil** sitting on a stone in the churchyard. On the stone is written: "Who so pulleth out this sword of this stone and anvil is rightwise king born of all England."

Arthur, the foster son of Sir Ector, works as a **page** for Ector's son Kay. He is helping Kay get ready when they discover that Kay's sword has been left at the lodging house. Arthur hurries back to fetch it, but the building is locked. Eager to help Kay, Arthur pulls the sword out of the stone in the churchyard and brings it to him. But when Kay sees it, he goes to his father and claims that he pulled the sword from the stone. Sir Ector makes Kay go back to the churchyard to show him how it was done. Kay soon confesses it was Arthur who pulled out the sword. When he slips it back into the stone, only Arthur can pull it out again.

Arthur is confused when Sir Ector and Sir Kay kneel down to him. What has happened? Sir Ector tells him about the night Merlin brought Arthur to him as a baby and asked the knight to raise him. Merlin never told him the boy was the secret son of Uther Pendragon. The other knights refuse to believe that Arthur is King Uther's son, and the heir to the throne. Test after test is held, but each time only Arthur can pull the sword from the stone. Finally, after weeks of arguing, the commoners demand that the knights end the delay and accept the boy. And so Arthur is crowned King of England.

Many Arthurian legends were about **quests** where knights set out to break evil spells and right wrongs. The most famous quest was for the **Holy Grail**. In early Christian times this was said to be the cup used by Jesus at the **Last Supper**. Only the purest of Arthur's knights, Sir Galahad, was able to succeed.

Beowulf

The epic poem *Beowulf* was written by an unknown English author around 700 CE. But the story it tells goes back hundreds of years earlier and across the sea to Scandinavia.

The Story of Beowulf and Grendel

Beowulf, the nephew of the king of Geatland in Sweden, has the strength of 30 men. But everyone thinks he's lazy, because he's never had to fight anything worse than a small dragon. One day he hears a **minstrel** sing about a monster called Grendel in Denmark. For 12 years Grendel has terrorized the drinking hall of Heorot, attacking the village and killing all the warriors. Beowulf decides to kill Grendel and save the Danes.

In Denmark, the hall of Heorot is filled with cobwebs and moss. The king welcomes Beowulf and his men, and holds the first feast in 12 years. Afterwards the Danes leave. Grendel sneaks up and casts a sleeping spell over Beowulf's warriors. But Beowulf resists, and wrestles the monster to the ground. He wrenches Grendel's arm off at the shoulder, and in the morning shows it to the amazed Danes.

But the next day the arm is gone and a friend of the king is found dead. Grendel's mother has come to take revenge. Beowulf tracks Grendel's mother to a foul lake spewing evil vapors. Fully armed, he sinks down into the muck to find Grendel's mother in her underwater **lair**. They struggle, but Beowulf finds a giant sword and kills her with it. Then he kills Grendel, lying in a corner. On shore his companions see blood in the water and think Beowulf is dead. But then he surfaces, holding the heads of Grendel and Grendel's mother in his hands.

It's set in Sweden and Denmark at a time when tribes of people were ruled by strong kings who kept peace and order by employing bands of warriors.

To ensure their loyalty, the kings would invite the warriors to feast with them in vast halls. They would pay the warriors with treasure captured in war. The warriors in turn would compete with one another to show their lord that they possessed the greatest bravery and strength.

Did You Know?

Very few people had ever heard of *Beowulf* until Oxford University Professor J.R.R. Tolkien wrote about it in 1936. Tolkien used his knowledge of Northern European mythology to write his own legendary novels, *The Hobbit* and *The Lord of the Rings*.

Norse Mythology

The Norse people came from Norway, Sweden, and Denmark. Each was a separate kingdom, but they were united by a shared mythology. They were farmers and excellent shipbuilders and sailors. Around 800 CE, they gave up farming and began raiding the northern coasts of Europe, terrifying the local people. Now known as the Vikings, they

Words to Know

quest: an adventurous journey in search of a specific goal.

Holy Grail: the legendary cup used by Jesus at the Last Supper. Searched for by knights in medieval legends.

Last Supper: in the Bible, the last meal Jesus eats.

minstrel: a performer who tells stories through song.

lair: hiding place.

snuck into towns on inland waterways by rowing their dragon-headed longships with their sails taken down. Eventually they controlled parts of Ireland, Scotland, England, and France. They are also the first Europeans known to have set foot on North America.

Thor is probably the best-known Norse god today. He had a belt that gave him magical strength, and his hammer made the thunder.

But there are many other colorful characters. Odin, also known as Woden, was the wisest and most powerful god. He had two ravens who brought him news of the world, and an eight-legged horse.

Loki, a shape-shifting trickster, comes from the race of frost giants. In one myth he causes the death of Balder the beloved, son of Odin and his wife Frigga. Tyr, the war god, lost a hand tying up Loki's demon wolf-son, Fenrir.

Norse myths featured trees, animals, giants, and dwarves, as well as gods and goddesses. A gigantic tree called Yggsdrasill connected nine worlds in its roots and branches. These included Asgard, the home of the sky gods; Hel, the home of the unworthy dead; and Midgard (Middle Earth), where humans dwelled. It was connected to Asgard by a rainbow bridge.

Tuesday, Wednesday, Thursday, and Friday are named after the Norse gods Tyr, Odin (or Woden), Thor, and Frigga. Sunday and Monday are from the sun and moon, and Saturday comes from the Roman god Saturn.

Most mythologies have stories about the creation of the world. Norse mythology also has a myth about how the world will end. That time is called Ragnarok, and—not surprisingly—it is said to be brought about by the trickster Loki.

Did You Know?

Valhalla was Odin's feasting hall in Asgard. Warriors were sent there when they died bravely in battle. Every day they got to fight again, training for the end-of-the-world battle of Ragnarok. Then the wounded or killed were restored in time for dinner.

Ragnorok, the End of the World

Frigga, the mother of Balder, wants to make her son immortal, like the mother of Achilles did. So she convinces everything on Earth—all the plants and animals—to promise not to harm him. The only thing she misses is the mistletoe vine.

Loki tricks Balder's blind brother Hoder into killing him with a mistletoe branch. The other gods catch Loki, tie him to a rock, and let a snake drip venom onto his face. But Loki escapes and leads an army of frost giants to Asgard to take revenge on the other gods. He is helped by his monstrous children: Hel, goddess of the underworld; the Midgard Serpent, which surrounds the human world; and the wolf Fenrir.

Loki storms the rainbow bridge, where his arch-enemy Heimdall is the sentry. Heimdall sounds the warning on his horn, calling the warriors from Valhalla to join the gods in battle. Then he and Loki fight and kill one another. Thor takes on the Midgard Serpent, which shakes the earth with its thrashing. He destroys the serpent, but dies from its poison.

Odin is ripped apart by Fenrir, and the giant wolf is killed by Odin's son, Vidar. Sol, the sun goddess, and her brother Mani, the moon god, are devoured by the giant wolf brothers Skoll and Hati. As the two armies fight to the end, the fire giant Surt burns up what is left of the nine worlds. The universe is plunged into darkness.

But that's not the end. Before she dies, Sol gives birth to a new sun goddess. A new earth rises from the sea. Odin's sons Vidar and Vali, and Thor's sons Modi and Magni, the only surviving gods, are joined by Balder and Hoder, who return from the dead. And two humans, Lif and Lifthrasir, emerge to start humankind again.

Make a Beltane Flower hair Wreath

Supplies

- 4 pipe cleaners
- wildflowers, with stems (real, artificial, or made from colored paper)
- twist ties or tape
- scissors
- ribbon

May Day celebrations are still held in former Celtic regions. Dancers weave colorful ribbons around a maypole and leap over bonfires. Girls and women decorate their hair with wreaths. This custom may be related to the Roman festival Floralia, honoring the goddess of flowers, as well as to Celtic tradition.

1 Connect the ends of two pipe cleaners to make one long strand. Repeat with other pipe cleaners.

2 Take the two long strands and loosely twist them together to make one double strand.

3 Bend the double strand into a circle that fits your head. Connect the ends. This is the framework of the wreath.

4 Cut the flowers so that about 2 inches (5 centimeters) of stem remains.

5 Weave the stems into the wreath framework. Secure with tape or twist ties. Trim off any wires sticking out.

6 Wrap the ribbon around the wreath, covering over the ends of the stems and any wires. Tie the ribbon in a bow and let the ends fall down the back.

Make a Celtic Triskeles Armband

The triskeles is a common Celtic design that looks like a wheel made of three running legs joined at the center. It is often used on pieces of fine metalwork. You can also use Celtic designs from shields or other objects as inspiration for your armband. You will be drawing on the back side, so your final design will be reversed on the front.

1 Make a pattern for your armband from scrap paper. Try it on to get it the size you want, and add about half an inch (1.25 centimeters). Cut this shape from your aluminum or copper and put it on the soft work surface.

2 Fold over the edges of your metal no more than half an inch. Press down smoothly with the back of a metal spoon or flat stick. Make sure no sharp edges stick out to cut you when you wear your armband.

3 With the folded-over edges facing you, draw your design on the armband. To make the design stand out more, turn the armband over and outline the design from the front too. Bend the armband to fit on your arm.

4 If you like, glue spangles or other decorations to the front of the armband. Let dry.

Make a British Sword in the Stone

1 Carve the Styrofoam into the shape of a stone with the knife.

2 Dab indentations in the stone with black paint. Mix some black and white paint to make grey. Paint the rest of the rock grey. Let dry.

3 Use the knife to make a slot for the sword.

4 Cut a rectangle the size of the sword you want to make from the cardboard. Cut two pieces of aluminum foil the same size.

5 Cover one side of the cardboard completely with glue stick. Smooth on one piece of aluminum foil. Repeat with other side.

6 With the pen, draw a sword shape on the aluminum foil-covered cardboard and decorate it. Carefully cut out the sword. Push it into the stone.

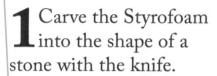
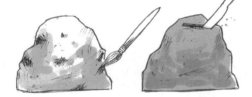

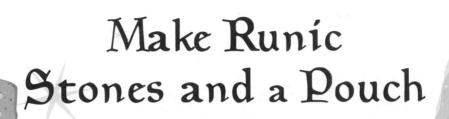

Make Runic Stones and a Pouch

The Vikings had a form of writing called runes that they believed had magical powers. Runic messages on swords asked the gods for protection or victory. Warriors put the symbol for Tyr, the god of war, on their shields. Runes appeared on large memorial stones that were historical and boundary markers. And small flat stones with runes painted on them were used to tell fortunes and cast spells. The stones were shaken up in a leather pouch and tossed on the ground, then read by special Rune Masters. Rune symbols probably came from other European alphabets. But in Norse mythology, the god Odin learned runes by sacrificing an eye in the Well of Knowledge at the root of Yggdrasill.

Supplies

- several small, smooth clean stones
- permanent marker
- bowl
- pen
- felt, leather, or other sturdy fabric
- scissors
- yarn or string

1 Draw a rune symbol on each stone with the permanent marker.

2 To make the pouch, use a bowl or other round object about 10 inches (25 centimeters) across to trace a circle on the felt with the pen. Cut out the circle.

3 Cut small holes around the edge of the circle about 2 inches (5 centimeters) apart with the scissors.

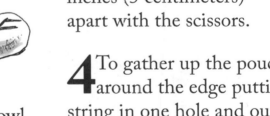

4 To gather up the pouch, go around the edge putting the string in one hole and out the next. Keep the ends on the outside of the pouch and knot them. Pull the string tight to close the pouch.

Chapter 5
Sub-Saharan Africa

The part of Africa that lies south of the Sahara Desert is made up of many different countries and cultures. Even today African tribes and ethnic groups are still important—sometimes more important than nationality when it comes to loyalty. Individual tribes often have their own mythic traditions, so there are lots of sacred stories to tell. But some stories, themes and characters appear over and over again around the continent.

Most African mythologies have one supreme being. After creating the world and humankind, this being often gets fed up with people and goes away. So most sacred stories are about less-powerful beings and **ancestor** spirits.

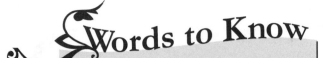

Words to Know

ancestor: people who came before you, like your grandparents.

yam: an edible root similar to a sweet potato.

Did You Know?

Twins appear often in African mythology. In most parts of the world, twins are relatively uncommon, with only four sets of twins born in every thousand babies. For the Yoruba, however, the number is much higher, with 45 sets of twins in every thousand babies born. Twins are considered to be the children of Shango and to have special powers. If one twin dies, the mother will carry around a small statue called an Ibeji to represent its soul.

Yoruba Mythology

In the mythology of the Yoruba people of Nigeria and Benin, the Supreme Being is called Olorun. The guardian spirits under his control are called the Orishas. There are hundreds of Orishas, including Babalu-Aye, the god of healing; Shango, the god of thunder; and Eshu, a messenger and trickster.

One day, the Orishas get together and try to force Olorun to give up his power for 16 years. Olorun agrees to step down and let them take over for 16 days. The Orishas last eight days as rulers of the universe before begging Olorun to return. Afterwards, they become his obedient servants. However, Eshu steals some **yams** and covers up the crime by making tracks with Olorun's sandals. When the people blame Olorun for the theft, he leaves Earth and makes Eshu his go-between.

In Yoruba history, Shango was the fourth king of the Oyo Empire.

This empire controlled part of West Africa from the 1400s to 1835 CE. According to Yoruba mythology, Shango became a god after his death. Yoruba priests sometimes use carvings of Shango wearing a two-headed "thunder axe" headpiece.

Bata Drum

Shango's special instrument is the double-headed Bata drum, which is shaped like an hourglass. Bata drums are used in sets of three, with each drum a different size: Iya ("the mother"), Iitotele ("he who follows in rank"), and Okonkolo ("the baby"). Each drum has its own pitch. The pitch is how high or low a musical note is. This makes it possible to use the drums to "speak" the Yoruba language, which uses different tones to indicate the meaning of a word.

The Yoruba use Bata drums for prayers, announcements, and even jokes or teasing. Strict rules control how Bata drums are made (the heads must be of special goat or deer skin) and who may play—or even touch—them. Today, Latin jazz and salsa bands in the Caribbean, South America, and the United States use non-sacred Bata drums to create their music.

The legend of Shango and many other Orishas were brought to the New World with African slaves. These myths formed the basis of **Voodoo** in Haiti and **Santeria** on Cuba.

The story of the Storm of Shango tells how Shango became the god of thunder and lightning. In another version of the myth, which may be closer to the truth, Shango's frustrated subjects chase him out of his kingdom. After Shango's death, his supporters burn down his enemies' homes, sparking the legend of his divine powers.

Words to Know

Voodoo: a religion based on Yoruba gods said to involve witchcraft.

Santeria: a religion that combines Yoruba gods, Roman Catholic saints, and animal sacrifice.

Did You Know?

Nigeria, the country where most Yoruba people live, is just north of the equator. In this area, strong winds and moist tropical air form tremendous thunderstorms. Nigeria has the second-highest number of thunderstorms in the world.

The Storm of Shango

King Shango is fascinated by deadly charms. One day, he discovers a spell to summon lightning, and decides to test it on his own dwelling. He calls his advisors to his home, and then utters the charm. A storm rises up, and lightening strikes his house. The lightning sets his house on fire, which destroys the house and Shango's entire family.

Having lost everything that he values, including his sons, Shango is overcome with grief and regret. He decides that he will leave the kingdom and rule no more. When he tells his advisors his plan, some say it is best. Others try to make him change his mind. Angry at their opposition to his will, Shango kills 160 of them: the 80 who disagreed too strongly, and the 80 who agreed too eagerly.

Then, with just a few friends, Shango departs his kingdom and starts a long journey. One by one, his friends desert him, until he is finally left all alone. Filled with despair, Shango decides to end his life and hangs himself from a tree. When his subjects learn of his death, they come to the place where he died, and bury him with all the honors that a king deserves. After that, whenever they hear thunder or see lightning in the sky, they know that Shango is making an angry judgment on them.

Make a Bata Thunder Drum

Supplies

- 2 yogurt containers or other cone-shaped plastic cups
- scissors
- masking or duct tape
- 2 latex balloons
- rubber bands
- colored tape, paint, feathers, sequins, other decorations
- glue
- spoon

Bata drums were brought by African slaves from Yorubaland. They became a central part of the Santeria religion on Cuba.

1 Cut off the bottoms of the containers. Then join the bottomless containers together with tape.

2 Cut off the bottoms of the balloons. Leave enough latex on the top of the balloons to stretch over the openings of the containers.

3 Stretch the balloons over the openings, and secure with rubber bands or tape.

4 Decorate the containers with colored tape, paint, feathers, sequins, and other decorations.

5 Try playing your drum, using the spoon as a drumstick. For a complete set of Bata drums, make two more drums, using different-sized containers.

Words to Know

pestle: a club-shaped stick for crushing food or medicine.

calabash gourd: a large, hard squash that is dried and used to make bottles.

Adinkra: Ashanti symbols that represent proverbs.

proverb: advice in the form of a well-known saying.

animist: a belief that objects and parts of nature have spirits.

Ashanti Mythology

Nyame is the Supreme Being of the Ashanti people of Ghana and the Ivory Coast. One myth about Nyame is similar to the story of the Tower of Babel in the Bible. Long ago, he lived in the sky, close to the people. However, he was driven away by a woman mashing yams with an African **pestle** tall enough to poke the sky. When Nyame moved to a higher level in the sky, the people tried to reach him by building a ladder of **calabash gourds**. However, the pile of gourds fell down, and Nyame stayed out of reach.

Trickster stories are common in African mythology. One popular Ashanti trickster is Anansi the spider. He is a greedy character who sometimes gets into trouble when he tries to grab too much. Many stories about Anansi came with African slaves to America.

Did You Know?

About a quarter of Africans in Ghana today believe in traditional **animist** religions.

The tales of the trickster Brer Rabbit in American author Joel Chandler Harris' book *Uncle Remus* are based on Anansi stories from Africa.

The Ashanti did not develop an alphabet, but they did create a system of symbols called **Adinkra**. Adinkra symbols are named after King Adinkra, an Ivory Coast king in the early 1800s. Each symbol stands for a **proverb** or saying. If you put them together, they make messages. The Ashanti use their Adinkra symbols to express ideas about the real and supernatural worlds.

Adinkra symbols are still used today on houses, pottery, and furniture. They are best known as designs on clothing. There are different types of Adinkra cloth, and special colors for different occasions. Red is for funerals, which are important, elaborate events in Ashanti culture. Multi-colored Adinkra cloth is worn on festive occasions. Chiefs have their own types of Adinkra as well.

Block printing is used to create Adinkra cloth. Symbols are carved into pieces of calabash gourd to make stamps. Handles for the stamps are several short sticks attached to the back. A thick dye is made by boiling the bark of the Kuntunki tree with iron **slag**. The stamps are dipped into the dye and then pressed into the cloth. The stamped images are square, repeated in a **grid** pattern to make the Adinkra design.

Words to Know

slag: ash left from burning metal.

grid: a pattern of identical boxes.

plantain: a type of banana tree with long flat leaves.

Anansi Gets Stories from Nyame

Anansi the spider wants all the stories of the world. However, Nyame, the Supreme Being, keeps them in a golden box next to his royal stool in the sky. Anansi climbs up to the sky on his web and asks Nyame to sell him the stories. Amused, Nyame tells him the price: he must capture Osebo the leopard, Mmoboro the hornet swarm, and Mmotia the spirit.

First, Asansi digs a pit near the leopard's lair and covers it with leaves. When Osebo goes out to get a drink, he falls into the trap. Next, Anansi takes a calabash of water and a **plantain** leaf to Mmoboro's nest. He covers his head with the leaf like an umbrella, sprinkles the water on the nest, and calls to the hornets to take shelter in his calabash from the rain. When the hornets are inside, he closes the top with his leaf, capturing them.

Finally, Anansi makes a little wooden doll and covers it with sticky sap. He sets the doll out with a bowl of mashed yams by a tree where spirits often gather to dance. Mmotia comes by and asks the doll for some of the yams. When the doll doesn't reply, she slaps its face in anger, and her hand becomes stuck to the sap. She slaps it with the other hand, and the same thing happens. Then she kicks at the doll with both feet and they become stuck too. Anansi takes Osebo, Mmoboro, and Mmotia back to Nyame. The god is impressed, and rewards Anansi with the stories. After that, they are always known as Spider Stories.

Make Ashanti Adinkra Cloth

Adinkra cloth is woven in strips that are sewn together. Each strip is divided into boxes separated by borders. For an authentic look, use smaller stamps to decorate the borders and larger stamps to fill in each box with a repeated symbol.

Supplies

- newspaper
- knife
- potato
- paper towels
- pencil
- paint
- paper or cloth to print on
- marker, stick

1 Cover your workspace with newspaper. Have an adult help you cut a potato in half. Pat the potato dry with the paper towels. Draw your Adinkra symbol on the cut side of the potato with a pencil.

2 Use the knife to carve around the outside of your design. The design should stick up higher than the rest of the surface. Create several different stamps.

3 To make an ink pad, pour some paint onto a folded piece of paper towel on the newspaper. Thin your paint with a little water in a cup if it is too thick. The paper towel should be soaked through with paint.

4 Press the potato stamp against the paper towel until the stamp is evenly covered with a thin layer of paint.

5 Press the stamp onto the paper or cloth. Print each symbol four times, two above and two below, to make a square. Then create a square of four different symbols next to the first.

6 Use a marker or a stick pressed onto the ink pad to draw boxes around each section of symbols. Add a border if desired.

Chapter 6
India and China

The mythologies of Asia contain hundreds of gods. These gods are concerned mainly with the right way to live, rather than how nature works. Many different traditions have developed in Asia. Over the centuries, these various traditions have blended together, taken on different forms, and spread to other parts of the world.

Hindu Mythology

The Hindu mythology of India is incredibly complicated. It is said to have 333 million gods and goddesses! Many are alternate versions of the Trimurti, the three deities of Hinduism.

The first of these is Brahma, the creator. He is the **personification** of Brahman, the **spiritual** energy of the universe. He is usually shown with four faces and four arms. The second is Vishnu, the protector. He fights evil in the world, and can appear as one of 10 **avatars**, including Krishna and Rama. His 10th avatar will not appear until the end of the world. The third is Shiva, the destroyer. He is often shown in statues dancing and waving his four arms in a vertical ring of fire.

Vishnu and Shiva are also considered to be part of Brahma. So in Hindu mythology, vast numbers can be combined into one.

Hinduism is based on **unity** and cycles. According to its creation story, the universe came into being when Brahma woke up, and it will last as long as one of his days: about four billion years. When Brahma goes to sleep again, the universe will fade away. However, it will be born again when he awakens, onward into eternity.

Hindus believe that humans have their own cycle of death and rebirth called **reincarnation**. People are reborn into a higher or lower **caste** in their next life. That caste depends on their actions and behavior, or **karma**, in their past life. Gods can even be reborn as humans. Because of this cycle, each individual must find their own right behavior, called **dharma**.

Did You Know?

Today the word avatar is used to mean an image or animated character that represents you in a digital environment, like a Wii Mii in a computer game or Instant Message buddy icon.

Words to Know

personification: a god or being that represents a thing or idea.

spiritual: relating to religion or sacred things.

avatar: a human form taken by a Hindu deity.

unity: many things made into one.

reincarnation: rebirth in a new body or form of life.

caste: a social class in Hindu society that once determined a person's job and position by birth.

karma: the actions that decide a person's next incarnation.

dharma: a person's duty to follow divine law.

The Hindu religion is practiced by 700 million people around the world.

The oldest stories in the Hindu tradition are the *Vedas*. These are sacred songs and hymns composed by the Aryan people of the Indus Valley between 1500 and 1000 BCE. They deal with the supreme Vedic gods: Indra, the god of war, fertility, and thunder; Agni, the god of fire; and Surya, the god of the sun.

The *Vedas* were first written down in the Sanskrit language around 800–900 BCE. Over time, the Hindu gods grew to overshadow the Vedic gods, although the Vedic gods remained an important part of Hindu mythology.

Kali

Devi and Ganesha

The gods' wives also appear in many Hindu myths in various forms. The goddess Devi is one of the oldest deities. She makes her first appearance in the *Vedas*. Her avatars include the warlike Durga and the horrific Kali, "the dark one." Kali is black, wears a necklace of skulls, and laps up blood with her long tongue. Devi is also known as Parvati, the wife of Shiva and the mother of Ganesha.

Ganesha has a big pot belly and the head of an elephant. According to different stories, Shiva accidentally lopped off his son's head and had it replaced with the first one available. Ganesha is the most popular Hindu god, because he is associated with good luck and wisdom.

Ganesha

After the *Vedas* came the two great epic poems of Hindu mythology, the *Mahabharata* and the *Ramayana*. These poems are full of adventure, with gods, demons, and heroes. They are the inspiration for many Indian works of art and literature, even in modern times.

The *Mahabharata* was written between 400 and 300 BCE. It is about the hero Arjuna and two noble families, the Pandavas and the Kauravas, who quarrel over their kingdom. The *Bhagavad-Gita*, one section of the poem, has become extremely popular.

The *Ramayana*, compiled between 400 BCE and 200 CE, tells the story of Rama, one of the avatars of Vishnu. Rama rescues his wife Sita, an avatar of Lakshmi, who is the goddess of wealth. She had been kidnapped by the demon king Ravana and taken to his kingdom, the island of Lanka.

Did You Know?

The Ramayana and other Hindu myths provide an endless source of stories for movies made in Bollywood, India's film capital. Bollywood is located in the city of Mumbai, which used to be called Bombay. The name is a take-off on America's film capital, Hollywood.

how Rama Saved Sita

Rama is searching for his wife Sita when he meets Hanuman, the monkey god. Hanuman asks Rama to help him kill his evil brother. Rama does, and in return, Hanuman joins Rama in his search for Sita. Hanuman even convinces the monkeys and the bears to assist, too.

The first task is to reach the island of Lanka. Since Hanuman is the son of the Wind God, he is able to just leap over the ocean. Hanuman finds Sita and gives her Rama's ring as a sign that he is coming for her. Then Rama and the animals build a bridge from India to Lanka.

Once the bridge is built, Rama's animal army attacks Ravana's demon army. In the meantime, Rama and Ravana duel it out. Every time Rama cuts off Ravana's head, Ravana grows another one. Eventually, Rama beats the demon king.

Rama's animal army spreads out and finds Sita. They bring her to Rama, but suddenly he's not sure he wants her back. He suspects she has been unfaithful to him with Ravana. Sita proves her loyalty by stepping into a funeral **pyre** and emerging unharmed. Rama begs Sita for forgiveness, she gives it to him, and the couple joyously reunites.

Rama

At last, Rama and his army set off for home, with Hanuman in the lead. As they cross the bridge back to India, it sinks beneath the waves, leaving just a line of rocky islands. The whole country comes out to greet them as they make their way back, passing through villages and towns. To light the divine couple's way, all of the people place little lamps on their doorsteps.

Hanuman

Words to Know

pyre: an outdoor fire used for burning a dead body in a funeral ceremony.

Make a Rangoli Design

Every fall, people in India celebrate a holiday called **Diwali,** or the Festival of Lights. They decorate the entrances of their homes with small clay lamps called diya. They also hang up paper chains and create colorful sand sidewalk designs called **rangoli.** These decorations are meant to invite Lakshmi, the goddess of **prosperity,** into their homes. Most rangoli are done inside a circular outline. Popular subjects include flowers, leaves, cows, elephants, horses, eagles, swans, butterflies, and geometric designs.

Supplies

- sidewalk or large piece of paper
- colored sidewalk chalk
- colored sand or rice (optional)
- hairspray or art fixative

1 Get permission to draw on the sidewalk, or use a large piece of paper. Use the colored chalk to draw the outlines of a rangoli design.

2 To fill in with color, start in the center and work your way towards the edges. Rub in more chalk, or carefully sprinkle colored sand or rice into the spaces.

3 To make your design last longer, spray with hairspray or art fixative. Only use spray outdoors or with windows open.

Words to Know

Diwali: the Hindu festival of lights celebrating the New Year.

rangoli: a geometric design drawn on the ground in front of a house.

prosperity: wealth.

Buddhist Mythology

Buddhism was founded by an Indian prince named Siddhartha Gautama, who became the Buddha around 500 BCE. Buddha believed there was a way to end Hinduism's eternal cycle of reincarnation. People who lived a good life could escape reincarnation and reach a state of **nirvana**.

Buddha gave up his family and position in society. He chose to live as simply as possible, without belongings or property. At first, Buddha's followers did the same. They became monks and nuns.

Words to Know

nirvana: the state of bliss that is the goal of Buddhism.

stupa: a dome-shaped Buddhist shrine, with a rounded top.

Buddhism began in India, but it became even more popular in other parts of Asia such as China and Japan.

Around 300 BCE, an Indian king named Ashoka, who was looking for an alternative to war, became a Buddhist. He made Buddhism the state religion, and helped spread it by building **stupas** across the country. Over time, however, most Buddhists in India went back to Hinduism, and brought Buddha with them into the Hindu pantheon of gods and goddesses.

Stupa

By the 600s CE Buddhism had been brought to China and other parts of Asia. Men and women adopted its teachings and entered Buddhist monasteries. But most people outside India practiced a less strict form of Buddhism. It allowed them to have jobs, families, and property.

Words to Know

fable: a story with a moral.
moral: a lesson about the right way to behave.

Eventually, there were more Buddhists in other countries than in India. In these areas, Buddhism combined with local religions to create new traditions.

In China, a collection of stories about Buddha's past incarnations called the *Jataka Tales* became popular. The 550 tales show Buddha as he appeared in past lives, sometimes in animal form. Each tale is a **fable** with a moral. Some scholars believe that *Aesop's Fables* are based on the *Jataka Tales*. For example, some versions of the Buddhist story *The Golden Swan* are very similar to Aesop's *The Goose That Laid the Golden Eggs*.

The Golden Swan

A swan with beautiful golden feathers sees a very poor woman and her daughters. He decides to help them, and flies to their house. He tells them to take one of his golden feathers. If they sell the feather, they can use the money to live.

When the money runs out, the swan returns and lets them take another feather. But the mother becomes worried. What if the swan changes his mind and doesn't come back one day? The next time the swan visits, she tells her daughters to catch him and pluck out all his feathers. The daughters refuse, but the greedy mother does it herself.

Now the swan must wait for his feathers to grow back before he can fly away. But when they do grow back they are no longer golden. They are plain white. This time, the swan flies away and never returns.

Make a Buddhist Stone Stupa

The original stupas were burial mounds of rock. Gradually they evolved into graceful dome-shaped structures. Some contain **relics**, while others are just **monuments**. Stupas are designed for **circumambulation**. As you walk around the base, a series of carvings or paintings show scenes from the life of Buddha. There is a Buddhist stupa called the Peace Pagoda in Grafton, New York, which is approached by a path through the woods. Visitors sometimes build miniature stupas from small rocks along the trail.

1 Find a place to build your stupa, like a garden, wooded area, or an indoor planter.

2 Carefully arrange the stones in a tall, narrow pile that is larger at the bottom and gets smaller as you go up. The stones must be well balanced so they don't come tumbling down. This takes patience.

Supplies

- stones of different sizes, but not too heavy to pick up
- hot-glue gun (for miniature stupas)

3 For a miniature stupa, hot-glue the stones in place and set into the planter.

Words to Know

relic: a sacred object connected with a holy person.

monument: a site or structure that has special meaning.

circumambulation: to walk around something in a ritual.

Chinese Mythology

Chinese mythology is a colorful blend of many separate traditions. The earliest stories, from around 2000 BCE, were about gods of the natural world, like the earth, the sun, and fire. Ruling over them all was the god Shang-Ti.

Shang-Ti was replaced by Tian around 1100 BCE. Tian was not a god, but rather an idea of heaven. It was usually pictured as a dome with a hole in the middle for the weather to come through.

Parents and grandparents were also considered gods when they died, and each family worshipped its own ancestors.

About 500 BCE, the **philosopher Confucius** came up with rules for an orderly society. These rules included respect for those in charge, whether parents, rulers, or gods. He also had rules for those in power. These rules told them how to govern wisely and fairly. The philosophy of Confucius became very popular with Chinese rulers, especially the part that told the people to obey those in charge.

Confucius

Words to Know

philosopher: someone who tries to understand and explain existence and reality.

Confucius: Chinese philosopher who founded Confucianism based on order.

philosophy: a way of thinking or set of beliefs.

Taoism: a Chinese philosophy and religion based on accepting the world.

qi: the life-force inside everything.

yin: the dark, passive female spirit.

yang: the light, active male spirit.

Communist: a type of government that includes, among other things, banning religion.

 **Did You Know?**

Emperors and empresses had to have the Mandate of Heaven to rule. If they lost it, they were overthrown by a new emperor or empress.

72

At the same time, Lao-Zi developed the **philosophy** of Tao, a librarian who worked for the emperor. **Taoism** said that **qi**, or the energy of the universe, flowed through all things. Lao-Zi's philosophy taught people to work with this force so they could find easy ways to achieve goals, rather than fighting and struggling. This idea was called wu-wei, or "doing by not doing."

Qi has two sides: **yin** and **yang**. In Taoism, yin and yang has to be kept in balance to stay healthy and function well.

At first, Confucianism and Taoism were codes to live by, not religions. But as these philosophies became more popular, their followers adapted some of the older myths to fit in with their new beliefs. New stories were also added.

Then, in the first century CE, Buddhism entered China from India. New Buddhist stories were created to appeal to Chinese ways of thinking. The idea of Tian was replaced with a new supreme god called the Jade Emperor. He spoke only to the emperor of China.

Ordinary Chinese people were under the supervision of lesser gods, the spirits of departed rulers, and other immortals. With the idea of reincarnation, supernatural record keepers were added to the pantheon. Their job was to keep track of each person's good and bad deeds. They even kept tabs on animals, who could come back as humans through good behavior.

Did You Know?

Many Chinese gods were based on actual historical figures, such as victorious generals. For instance, the Taoist god of war, Guan-Yu, was a general of the Han Dynasty around 200 BCE.

This combination of Chinese nature mythology, Confucianism, Taoism, and Buddhism created a unique culture. Today there is officially no religion in China, according to the **Communist** Chinese government. But Chinese sacred stories and customs still survive.

A Chinese Creation Myth

Inside a Cosmic Egg, chaos reigns. Then chaos separates into yin and yang. The Egg hatches, and out comes Pan-gu, the primal giant. As Pan-gu grows, he pushes the heavy yin down and the lighter yang up. Eventually, Pan-gu tires and dies, and from his body grow trees, grass, rivers, oceans, and rock.

Then the first beings appear on Earth. Fu Xi and his sister Nu-Gua are human, but have the tails of serpents. Nu-Gua becomes lonely, and creates some humans out of clay. She designs them carefully, giving them legs instead of snakes' tails.

The next day, she decides to try a faster way of making people. This time, she drags a cord through the mud. When she flings the cord around, the mud goes flying. The splatters of mud become more people. However, the mud people are not as well-made as the clay people. The clay people become the nobles and the mud people become the peasants. Nu-Gua marries Fu Xi, who serves as the first emperor and teacher of mankind.

Other gods appear, including Gong Gong, the god of water, and Zhu Rong, the god of fire. Water and fire fight to rule the universe, but Gong Gong loses. In a rage, he bangs his head against Imperfect Mountain, which holds up the sky. Floods of water pour down from the hole in Tian, and the people Nu-Gua created are in danger of drowning. Nu-Gua patches up the hole with molten rocks, and then she props up the sky with the legs of the Celestial Tortoise. In this way, Nu-Gua, creator of the human race, also becomes its savior.

Did You Know?

In Chinese mythology, four spiritual creatures called celestial emblems guarded the directions of the compass. The celestial black tortoise represented north, as well as winter. The celestial white tiger represented west and the season of fall, the celestial red bird south and summer, and the celestial blue dragon east and the season of spring.

Make a Magic Square

In one Chinese myth, Fu-Xi, who is also the god of creativity, discovers a pattern of numbers with magical properties. It appears to him as a design of lines and dots on the shell of the Celestial Tortoise. This pattern is called a lo-shu. It is a type of math puzzle known as a Magic Square. In a Magic Square, every row and column of numbers, both across and down, adds up to the same total. In more complicated squares, even the diagonals and/or other combinations of boxes do this. There are also Magic Squares that use multiplication or even the number of letters in the name of the number!

Supplies

- paper
- pencil

The original Magic Square discovered by Fu-Xi used the numbers from 1 to 9. Every direction (including diagonals) adds up to 15. Here's how to make a nine-box Magic Square, starting with any number and going up in order.

1 Draw a square and divide it into nine boxes, with three rows and three columns. Now fill in the boxes following the letters on the diagram in order. For the first box, choose any number and put it in the box marked "A."

2 Take the next number in order and put it in the box marked "B." Continue filling in the numbers in order. For instance, if you put 7 in the "A" box, you should put 8 in the "B" box, 9 in the "C" box, and so on.

3 See what other arrangements you can come up with. Cut apart the rows and put them in a different order. Does the Magic Square still work? What if you double every number? Can you multiply one Magic Square by another? The more you play with it, the more magic the square becomes!

Make a Chinese Wind Goddess Tiger Kite

Supplies

Supplies

- paper lunch bag
- markers
- 2 bamboo barbecue skewers
- wire cutters or scissors
- ribbon or strip of plastic garbage bag
- crochet thread or kite string
- craft stick

Kites were most likely invented in China around 1000 BCE. They were originally used by the military to send messages. They also became popular as toys, and as a way to send away bad luck or to contact the gods.

Feng-po is the goddess of wind who rides a giant tiger through the air. Over her back, she carries a large bag. When she wants the wind to blow from a certain direction, she points the opening of the bag that way and opens it.

1 Draw a kite on the paper bag. Add a Feng-po flying tiger design. Cut out the kite.

2 Punch holes in the kite with the pointed end of the bamboo skewer. Thread the skewers through the holes, horizontal skewer first.

3 With the wire cutters, carefully snip off any extra skewer. Leave a half inch (1 centimeter) of skewer on the bottom.

4 Make a tail from the ribbon or the strip of plastic bag. Tie the tail to the bottom of the stick at the back of the kite.

5 Tape one end of the thread to the craft stick. Wind the rest around the stick. Tie the other end of the thread to the crossed skewers at the front of the kite.

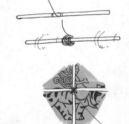

Chapter 7
Japan and Australia

Japan is a string of islands in the Pacific Ocean, but it is strongly tied to the rest of Asia. Its population and its sacred traditions both started out as transplants from Korea and China. Australia was once connected to the rest of Asia by strings of islands. When ocean levels rose at the end of the last Ice Age, Australia was left by itself in the south. Because of this the wildlife and the people of Australia developed in unique ways.

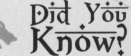

Did You Know?

The first people to inhabit Japan were the Ainu. The Ainu may be distant relatives of the Aborigines of Australia.

World Myths and Legends

Despite their differences, Japan and Australia share mythologies that consider the land, and all the living things on it, to be infused with supernatural spirits.

Japanese Mythology

Japan's earliest sacred tradition is Shinto, and its gods are called kami. There are kami for everything in the natural world: trees, rivers, mountains, and even people. The many Shinto gods were catalogued by a servant of the empress in 712 CE. This catalog is called the *Kojiki*, or *Record of Ancient Things*.

In Shinto mythology, the volcanoes of Japan are sacred places. Mount Fuji, the highest mountain in Japan, is the home of the goddess Sengen-Sama. According to legend, she knocks down climbers who don't approach her with proper respect.

Did You Know?

Japan was once called the "Land of the Rising Sun," because it was believed to be as far east as anyone could go. The Japanese flag shows a red sun, and before World War II also had rays of sunshine coming out of it.

Buddhism arrived in Japan in the sixth century CE. Confucianism and Taoism soon followed, although they were less popular in Japan than in China. But, just like in China, these different traditions came together and were transformed. Buddhists adopted the kami as various forms of Buddha. Today, many Japanese people observe a mix of Shinto and Buddhist customs. Some have even added customs from other traditions that appeal to them, such as Christmas celebrations.

Did You Know?

The Academy Award-winning children's animation, "Spirited Away" is about a little girl who must go to work in a bathhouse used by kami. It is just one of Japanese director Hayao Miyazaki's movies featuring characters from Shinto mythology.

A Japanese Creation Myth

At first, the world is an oily mass floating on the ocean like a jellyfish. Then the gods create two divine beings, Izanami and Izanagi, and give them the task of making the land. The pair stand on the Floating Bridge of Heaven and stir the waters with a jeweled spear. The drops that fall from its tip become the island of Onogoro. Here they build a palace where Izanami gives birth to the other islands, and the kami who rule them. But she dies giving birth to the fire god Kagutsuchi.

Heartbroken, Izanagi goes to Yomi, the Land of Darkness, to bring Izanami back. She warns him not to look at her, as she has already eaten the food of the dead. Yet he does, and when he beholds her rotting corpse he runs away in horror. Izanami gives chase, but Izanagi manages to seal her in with a giant boulder just in time. Enraged, Izanami vows to kill 1,000 humans a day in revenge. In turn, Izanagi vows to create 1,500 new people every day. Izanami becomes the goddess of death, and Izanagi the god of life.

Back from the underworld, Izanagi purifies himself with a cleaning ritual. As he washes his eyes he creates Amaterasu, the goddess of the sun, and Tsuk-Yumi, the god of the moon. From his nose he creates Susanowo, the storm god. But Susanowo is jealous of Amaterasu, and his angry outbursts drive Amaterasu into hiding in the Heavenly Rock Cave.

Without the sun, the world is plunged into darkness. So the other deities gather to lure her out. They hang a magic mirror from a tree facing the mouth of the cave. Then Uzume, the goddess of dance, performs and makes all the gods laugh. When Amaterasu peeks out to see what is going on, Uzume tells her they've found a new deity who outshines the sun. Amaterasu sees her image in the mirror and steps out to confront the new goddess. Quickly the other gods close off the mouth of the cave with a magic rope, so Amaterasu can never hide again.

Amaterasu

Make a Japanese Daruma Egg Doll

The name "daruma" comes from the Buddhist word dharma. Dharma is the truth about the way things are and will always be in the universe or in nature. According to legend, a Buddhist monk sat for so many years meditating that his arms and legs stiffened up. From then on, he rolled from place to place spreading the teachings of Buddha. In Japan, people buy daruma dolls on New Years' for good luck. The dolls come with blank eyes. To make a wish, you put a dot in the daruma's left eye. If it comes true, you fill in the other eye.

Supplies

- two-piece hollow plastic egg
- putty or non-drying clay
- red and white paint
- paintbrushes
- black permanent marker
- (optional) gold marker

1 Open the plastic egg. Stick the putty inside to the bottom of the big end. Close the egg and make sure it stands upright. If not, spread the clay around until it's balanced.

2 Open it again, place it open side down, and paint the bottom half of the egg red. Be careful not to paint inside the edges. Let dry.

3 Close the egg and stand upright. With the marker draw the outline of the face. Paint the face white and the rest of the body red. Let dry.

4 Draw the face over the white paint (See example.) Draw stripes on the body with the black or gold marker. Leave the eyes blank until you are ready to make a wish.

Words to Know

Southern Hemisphere: the half of the earth south of the equator.

clan: extended family group.

hunter-gatherers: people who get their food by hunting, fishing, and gathering wild plants instead of farming.

Australian Mythology

Australia is a country in the **Southern Hemisphere** that is also a continent. It consists mostly of deserts and open plains. Australia's first inhabitants are known as the Aborigines. They were the only people in Australia until Europeans arrived in 1606 CE. The Aborigines may have originally come from Southeast Asia between 50,000 and 65,000 years ago. That's when the last Ice Age caused the oceans to drop and land bridges to form between islands.

Traditionally the Aborigines lived in small **clans** of 50 to 500 people. These clans were part of larger groups, each with its own language. At one time about 700 different languages were spoken in Australia. The Aborigines were **hunter-gatherers** who had few manmade objects aside from tools and weapons made from sticks and stones.

🌿 Uluru

One of Australia's most famous landmarks is Uluru, or Ayer's Rock. This solid sandstone outcropping in the middle of the desert is sacred to several Aboriginal clans, who share control of the site with the Australian government. The climbing path to the top used by tourists is the traditional route used in Aborigine ceremonies. The local Aborigines do not forbid climbing but ask visitors to do the base walk instead, where they can see centuries of cave paintings layered upon each other.

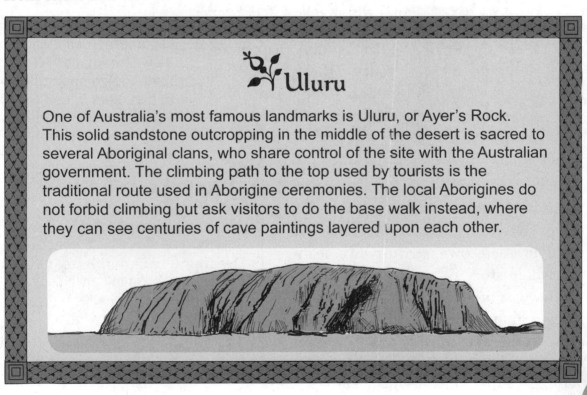

The Aborigines lived by catching kangaroos, **emus**, and turtles and collecting fruits, berries, and other plants. To avoid wiping out all the edible plants and animals in one area, they would travel around their territory. Sometimes they hunted with their neighbors, but generally clans stayed within their own territory. Borders were marked by rivers, lakes, and mountains.

The basis of Aborigines' mythology is called the **Dreaming** or the **Dreamtime**.

The Dreamtime contains their knowledge of the land, customs, and laws. The stories tell how ancestor spirit beings moved across the land in the form of humans or animals. Where they stopped, they created living things and features of the land. Once their work was done, the ancestor spirits changed again into animals or stars or hills or other objects.

The Dreamtime is both something that happened long ago and something that is still happening today. The places that appear in Dreaming stories are still sacred to the Aborigines, and some still perform rituals to honor them. The Dreamtime does not end, but is everlasting.

Each Aborigine clan has its own set of Dreaming stories that take place in their own territory. To learn the whole story of a Dreamtime hero, you have to literally follow his footsteps from region to region. There are also some stories that are only told by certain groups, such as older people or women.

Did You Know?

One Dreamtime story from southern Australia tells how Darama, the Great Spirit, took a spear thrown at him, bent it, and threw it back. It became the first boomerang.

Words to Know

emu: a bird similar to an ostrich but smaller.

Dreaming or **Dreamtime:** the time of creation in the mythology of the Australian Aborigines.

initiation: a ceremony where a member of a group is given special privileges.

Some areas can only be visited by certain people, such as the men of a clan. As the Aborigines go through life, they learn more and more of the Dreamtime stories. **Initiation** ceremonies and other rituals mark when they are ready to receive new knowledge.

The Aborigines preserved and passed along their sacred stories through oral traditions. They also told them through artwork, such as cave paintings, sand drawings, and drawings made on bark. One style of Aborigine art, X-ray painting, shows the inside of a human or animal. Another style was dot paintings. They were made on the ground and looked like maps. Special symbols showed footprints of people and animals. Rivers, mountains, and other landscape features appeared. The paintings showed the stories connected with a particular place.

When the English took over Australia starting in 1788 CE, they tried to wipe out Aborigine culture. Today, however, with new support from the Australian government, many Aborigines still hold on to their original beliefs.

❧ A Rainbow Serpent Creation Myth

In the Dreamtime, the Rainbow Serpent is sleeping underground when she awakens and pushes her way to the surface. As she slithers along the ground she leaves winding tracks. She makes deep hollows where she stops to sleep.

The Rainbow Serpent invites the frogs to awaken and join her. Their bellies are full of water that they have stored for the dry season. The Rainbow Serpent tickles them and they laugh, and the water pours out of their mouths. The water fills the Rainbow Serpent's tracks and hollows. Lakes fill up and rivers flow. Plants begin to grow, and other animals awaken to follow the Rainbow Serpent as she travels.

Make an Indoor Boomerang

Boomerangs are Aborigine throwing sticks, used for hunting and for sport. They are carved from bent sticks, so that they look and spin like airplane propellers. The spinning motion makes them travel in an arc that returns to the thrower. Here's how to make an indoor boomerang that really comes back.

Supplies

- stiff, light cardboard
- ruler
- scissors
- stapler
- markers

1 Cut two strips of cardboard, each about 1 inch (2.5 centimeters) wide by 8 inches (20 centimeters) long.

2 Round off the edges. Then fold up the tips about 1 inch (2.5 centimeters) from each end.

3 Staple the strips together in an X shape. Decorate with drawings in X-ray or dot painting style.

4 To throw, hold the boomerang vertically by one arm so that the folded tips are pointing towards you. Fling your hand forward like you are knocking on a door. The boomerang should glide around in a circle and come back to you.

5 You can experiment with different sizes, shapes, and weights of cardboard.

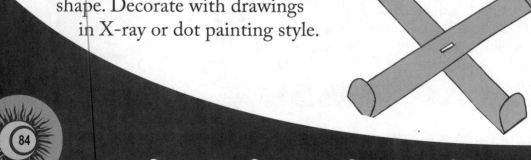

Chapter 8
Central and South America

In ancient times several great empires ruled parts of Mexico, Central America, and South America. They built enormous cities with high stone temples. They developed a **pictographic** form of writing. They made calendars that were extremely accurate. They kept records with a system of strings and knots. And they created colorful, if sometimes bloody, mythologies.

Words to Know

pictographic: using pictures instead of letters to write.

conquistador: Spanish conqueror.

missionary: someone sent to another country to spread their religion to the people there.

codex: an ancient sacred book.

Spanish Inquisition: a court where people were put on trial for breaking church law.

Did You Know?

Nobody knows who built it, but the ancient Mexican city of Teotihuacan was once the sixth-largest city in the world. It had a main street known as the Avenue of the Dead, immense pyramids, and temples with underground caves that were used as tombs.

The great Maya Civilization covered Mexico and Guatemala. It reached its height between 300 and 900 CE. Then, for reasons that are not known, it slowly faded. By 1200 CE, many of its great cities were nothing more than ruins in the jungles. Not long after, the Aztecs rose to power in Mexico. They took over parts of the Maya's former territory, and much of their culture. Meanwhile, in South America, the Incas were conquering their neighbors all around the Andes Mountains of Peru.

There is much we still don't know about the myths and legends of America's original civilizations.

Then, in the 1500s CE, **conquistadors** invaded Central and South America. Within a few short years they had destroyed the existing civilizations. Christian **missionaries** arrived and replaced native mythologies with European images and stories. But Christian scholars also preserved some of the native culture by recording what they heard and saw in writings and drawings.

Did You Know?

In 2008, a Mexican archaeologist found a series of caves that may be the route to Xibalba described in the *Popol Vuh*. The caves contained underground lakes littered with ancient Maya altars, pottery, and skulls. One chamber, studded with sharp stone points on its walls and ceiling, may be the "room of knives" mentioned in the story of the Hero Twins.

Tlachtli

Maya Mythology

The sacred book of the Maya was the *Popol Vuh*. It contains their creation myths and the family trees of their rulers. It also tells the story of the Hero Twins, Hunahpu and Ixbalanque. In the *Popol Vuh* they play an ancient Maya ball game called *ullamalitztli*.

The game was played on a ball court with high stone walls called a *tlachtli*. The goal of the game was to get the ball through the team's stone ring using only their elbows, knees, hips, and head. *Tlachtlis* were built next to Maya (and later Aztec) temples. They were considered portals to the underworld. Some experts believe the losing team was sacrificed.

What is a Codex?

The Maya made a type of folding book called a **codex** from the inner bark of trees. Codices (the plural) were used for writing about religion, astronomy, agricultural cycles, history, and prophecies.

The Maya wrote in pictographs, which were pictures representing words and sounds. They were very much like the hieroglyphics used by the Egyptians. Codices were sacred, and could only be read by priests after special purification rites. Spanish church officials destroyed most of the codices they found, but a handful were hidden and have survived.

Did You Know?

The scientist who discovered the caves that may be of the *Popul Vuh* made his discovery using trial records from the **Spanish Inquisition**. The trials were held in the 1500s by the Catholic Church to force the Maya to reveal the secret sites of their ancient ceremonies.

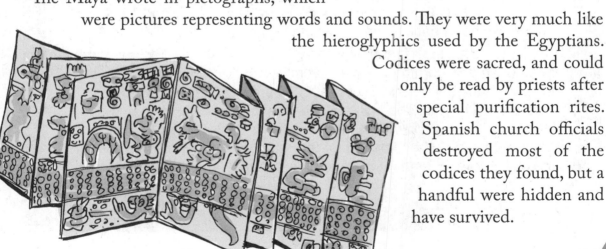

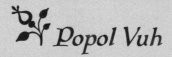

Popol Vuh

Hun Hunahpu, the god of fertility, and his brother Vucub Hunahpu are playing ball when their noise disturbs the Lords of Xibalba. These are the gods of the underworld. The gods challenge the brothers to a game, but first the brothers must survive certain challenges. The brothers must find their way through six rooms. The first is filled with darkness, the next cold, then jaguars, bats, knives, and fire. But the brothers fail the tests, and the next morning the Lords of Xibalba sacrifice the brothers on the ball field.

After the sacrifice, the gods hang Hun Hunahpu's head from a tree. There Ixquic, the daughter of one of the Lords of Xibalba, mistakes it for a fruit. When she tries to pick it, the head spits in her hand. Nine months later, Ixquic gives birth to Hun Hunahpu's sons, the Hero Twins Hunahpu and Ixbalanque.

Years pass, and Hunahpu and Ixbalanque learn to play ball. And they too are asked to play ball with the Lords of Xibalba. Unlike their father and uncle, however, they are prepared for the tests ahead of them. Even so they are stopped when Hunahpu loses his head in the chamber of bats. When it's time for the game, the Lords of Xibalba use Hunahpu's head as the ball. But Hunahpu manages to distract the gods and snatch his head back in time to win the game.

The gods try to defeat the Hero Twins one more time by luring them to an oven and burning them as sacrifices. But the boys use magic to come back to life. The Lords of Xibalba demand to know how this was done. They ask the twins to sacrifice them and bring them back to life the same way. However, the Hero Twins leave the gods dead and destroy Xibalba. Then, instead of returning to Earth, the twins rise into the sky. There, Hunahpu becomes the sun and Ixbalanque becomes the moon.

Play a Maya Ball Game

A version of the ancient ball game described in the *Popul Vuh* called *ulama* is still played today in some Mexican communities. Like its ancient form, it has complicated rules and ways of scoring and is very hard to play. The ball, called an *ulli*, is made of solid rubber, weighs 9 pounds, and can cost as much as $1,000. Players use their hips to hit the ball back and forth across a field. See if you can get a Maya-style volley going with your friends.

Supplies

- 2 or more players
- soccer or playground ball
- dirt or grass field

1 Draw a line between your side of the field and the other side.

2 To start the volley, stand with your shoulder facing the line. Take the ball and give it a smack with your hip so it goes over the line.

3 The player or players on the other side should try to hit the ball back to your side of the court using only their hip.

4 See how long you can keep the ball going back and forth over the line without letting it touch the ground.

Aztec Mythology

The Aztec empire ruled most of Mexico from 1325 to 1521 CE. Their capital city Tenochititlan was built on an island in the middle of Lake Texcoco in what is now Mexico City. The city was connected to the mainland by causeways, and crops grew in floating gardens on the lake.

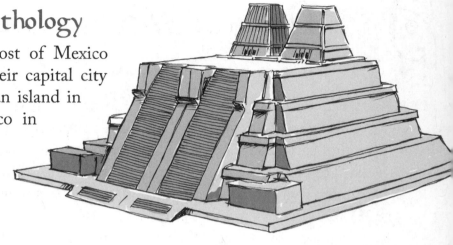

Tenochititlan Pyramid

In its center was the Great Temple, a double pyramid with two shrines. They were dedicated to Tlaloc, the god of rain, and Huitzilopochtli, the god of war.

The myths of the Aztecs, perhaps even more than those of other cultures, were filled with gruesome stories of fighting and sacrifice.

Tlaloc was an angry god who could send blight, frost, or total destruction, as well as rain. Huitzilopochtli carried the souls of dead warriors, in the form of hummingbird feathers, tied around one leg.

Huitzilopochtli's mother was the Earth goddess Coatlcue, who wore a skirt of snakes and a necklace made of human hands and hearts. When Coatlcue became pregnant with Huitzilopochtli by swallowing a feather, her daughter Coyolxauhqui and her 400 sons cut off her head.

 **Did You Know?**

In one myth, Huitzilopochtli tells the Aztecs to build their capitol city, Tenochititlan, where they see an eagle with a snake in its mouth, sitting on a cactus growing out of a rock. This image appears on the Mexican flag today.

Like Athena springing from the head of Zeus in Greek mythology, Huitzilopochtli emerged from his mother's dead body fully armed. Huitzilopochtli cut off his sister's head and transformed it into the moon. He killed his 400 brothers and turned them into the stars, and he himself became the sun.

The other major Aztec god was Huitzilopochtli's brother Quetzalcoatl, or "Feathered Serpent." The god of wind, Quetzalcoatl had a snake's body, but was kind and good. In Aztec stories, he often fights with another brother, Tezcatlipoca, or "Smoking Mirror," the god of death and temptation. Tezcatlipoca had a mirror in which he could see what others were thinking. In one tale, he changes Quetzalcoatl into a man.

Huitzilopochtli

❧ An Aztec Creation Myth

In Aztec mythology, the earth has been created and destroyed four times before the present period. Each era is called a "sun." Tezcatlipoca rules the First Sun until Quetzalcoatl throws his brother into the water and **jaguars** devour the earth. Quetzalcoatl rules the Second Sun, until Tezcatlipoca pushes him off his throne and he's blown away by a hurricane. The rain god Tlaloc rules the Third Sun, until Quetzalcoatl returns to destroy the earth with fiery rain. Tlaloc's wife, Chalchiuhtlicue, the goddess of water, rules the Fourth Sun. This sun ends with a giant flood, in which mankind is turned into fish. The fire god Xiuhtecuhtli rules the Fifth Sun, the present day. This sun will end with earthquakes.

Words to Know

jaguar: a large wild cat from Central and South America with yellow fur and black spots.

Words to Know

quetzal: a Central American bird with green and red feathers and a long tail.

appease: to satisfy with sacrificial offerings.

When Cortes first arrived in 1519, Tenochititlan may have been the largest city in the world.

There are varying stories of Quetzalcoatl's death. In one, he loses an argument with Tezcatlipoca and sets himself on fire. **Quetzal** birds fly out of the flames and Quetzalcoatl's heart becomes the morning star, the planet Venus.

In another version, Quetzalcoatl sails away to the east on a raft of serpents, promising to return. Some historians believe that when the Spanish conquistador Hernan Cortes arrived from the east in 1519, the Aztecs welcomed him because they thought he was the returning Quetzalcoatl.

The Gory Details of human Sacrifice

The Aztecs kept the gods **appeased** through human sacrifice. Different gods demanded different types of sacrifices. During some sacrifices, the Aztecs cut out the still-beating hearts of the victims. In others, they treated the victims as gods, giving them the best food, clothing and other luxuries for weeks or even months, until they eventually killed them. When Aztec priests wanted Tlaloc to provide rain for the crops, they chopped off the heads of crying children. The harder the children cried, the better they thought the yield of rainfall would be!

To ensure that Huitzilopochtli would carry the sun into the sky every morning, the Aztecs sacrificed one person every day. However, the Aztecs often sacrificed many more. During one ceremony in 1487 CE, the Aztecs sacrificed approximately 80,000 victims—prisoners captured from neighboring tribes—to the sun god in four days.

Make an Aztec Day of the Dead Calavera

Supplies

- 1 cup (250 milliliters) flour
- ⅓ cup (70 milliliters) water
- ⅓ cup (70 milliliters) salt
- oven
- glue and water
- permanent markers

The Day of the Dead, the most important holiday in Mexico, goes back to the Aztecs. Families decorate their homes with food, flowers, and other decorations, including happy skulls made of sugar called *calaveras*. They are not considered scary or sad, but represent the spirits of departed ancestors who have returned to visit. The Aztecs celebrated this day in August, but today it is held the day after Halloween, November 1. Have an adult help you make this version using homemade modeling dough dried in the oven.

1 Mix flour, water, and salt in a bowl. Add more water if the dough is too dry, or flour if it's sticky.

2 Form the dough into a ball. Squeeze it and mold it until it is smooth and stretchy.

3 Make the dough into an oval about 1 inch (2.5 centimeters) thick. Use your fingers, modeling tools, or a spoon to shape it into a skull.

4 Dry in the oven at 250 degrees Fahrenheit (120 degrees Celsius). After 30 minutes, check to see if the bottom is dry. If not, continue baking for 10 minutes until dry. Don't let the dough turn brown. Let cool.

5 Use markers to add details and designs. To preserve the skull, thin some white glue with water and paint it over the skull.

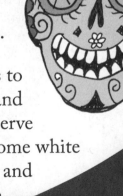

Incan Mythology

The Incan Empire was founded in Cuzco, Peru, around 1200 CE. By the 1400s, the Incas controlled much of the Andes Mountains of South America. To hold onto their vast lands, the Incas developed highly organized systems of transportation, communication, farming, and government. They built roads using tightly fitted stones that can still be seen today. They established an official language used by everyone for business. They designed **irrigation** systems and terraced fields to grow crops in desert and mountain areas. And they formed a group to control the supply of food and other goods.

In 1438, an emperor named Pachacuti came into power. Pachacuti rebuilt the capital city of Cuzco and reorganized Incan mythology around the sun god Inti. He claimed Inti's son Manco Capoc as his ancestor, making himself divine.

The Roads of the Incas

Incan roads were vital for connecting the vast empire across difficult mountainous terrain. They were used by traveling royalty and government officials, by armies on the march, and by trains of **llamas** carrying goods. Ordinary people needed special permission to use the roads.

The roads also helped the empire communicate. Special messengers called *chasquis* were stationed in huts every few miles along the road. When a message came through they would run to the next hut and tell it to the next *chasqui*, who would take it to the hut after that. Using this system of runners a message could be carried 150 miles (240 kilometers) a day.

Words to Know

irrigation: bringing water to the land to grow crops.

llama: a member of the camel family from the Andes with a long neck, long fur, and small head. Used for wool and to carry supplies.

Pachacuti also adopted the creation myth of an older god called Viracocha. In the Viracocha creation myth, the god made a race of giants out of stone. But the giants didn't obey him, so he turned them back into stone. In one version, he sent a flood to destroy them.

Next Viracocha made a better race of people from clay and commanded the sun, moon, and stars to appear. Viracocha sent his people to the earth's surface, then traveled around shaping the land and teaching them how to live. When he was through, Viracocha set off on a raft across the Pacific Ocean.

Creation of the Incan Empire

The sun god Inti sends out his four sons and four daughters to create a new empire, but they do not all succeed. Cachi, the oldest, becomes so troublesome that his brothers lock him away in a cave. The second oldest, Ucho, is transformed into a stone idol. The third oldest, Sauco, joins a group of peasants to teach them how to farm. However, Manco Capoc, the youngest, heads into the mountains with his sisters to find the perfect site for the new empire.

When Manco's magic golden rod sinks into the ground, he knows he has found the place for the empire. The wind is so strong that he can't construct any buildings. So he cages the wind in a llama pen. Within a short time, his brother Sauco comes along to tell him that he must let the wind go before the day ends. Manco has to find a way to make the day last long enough for him to build his city. He weaves a very strong rope and wraps it around the sun. Then he ties the other end to the top of a mountain. In this way, Manco keeps the sun from moving until he has finished his city and surrounded it with mountains. His empire complete, he then releases the sun and wind.

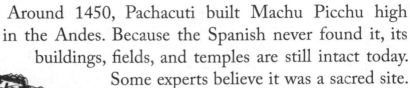

Around 1450, Pachacuti built Machu Picchu high in the Andes. Because the Spanish never found it, its buildings, fields, and temples are still intact today. Some experts believe it was a sacred site. Others think it was a retreat for the emperor and his court. A stone pillar called the Hitching Post of the Sun may have been used in ceremonies to symbolically tie the sun to the earth with a mystical cord. It may be related to the myth about Manco Capoc, the son of the sun god and legendary ancestor of the Inca emperors.

Did You Know?

The Incas had large stores of gold, but they did not use money. Instead of collecting taxes to help build the empire, they required all married men to spend a certain amount of time each year doing work for the government.

After Pachacuti, other rulers extended the Incan Empire into Chile, Bolivia, Argentina, Colombia, and Peru. By 1527, it may have been the largest nation in the world. Like the Aztecs, the Incan empire came to an end when Spanish conquistadors arrived. In 1532, the Incas welcomed Francisco Pizarro as the incarnation of Viracocha. With only 260 well-armed men, Pizarro defeated 7,000 Inca warriors, captured the emperor, and took over the empire.

Incan Mummies

The Incas had mummies, too. Unlike the Egyptians, mummification wasn't only for rulers, and mummies weren't kept in huge tombs. Many Incan mummies were children who were sacrificed to Viracocha. After an elaborate ceremony, the Incans would take the children high into the mountains and leave them to freeze to death in stone enclosures. Archaeologists are still finding perfectly-preserved ice mummies today.

Make an Incan *Quipu*

The Incas had a unique tool for recording information called a *quipu*. A *quipu* was a long string with shorter strings of different colors hanging off it. The shorter strings had various knots tied in them at specific points. The different knots and colors made up a code that could be read by trained officials called *quipucamayocs*. *Quipus* were used for keeping government records and sending messages. Many archaeologists believe the *quipus* were also used as a way to "write down" myths and stories. When the Spanish arrived they destroyed most of the *quipus* they found, but about 700 still exist. Scientists are using computers to try to decode the *quipus* and reveal their mysteries.

Supplies

- different colors of string or yarn
- scissors

In this activity, you'll record secret messages with only colors and a few varieties of knots.

1 Decide on a code for your *quipu*. Assign a color of string to something you want to keep track of. For instance, you can add up how many comic books you own, or how many minutes you spent exercising.

2 Cut a long piece of string to use as your main cord.

3 To make a hanging cord, take a piece of string and double it, making a loop. Wrap the loop around the middle of the main cord. Pull the ends through the loop as shown until tight.

4 Do the same with the rest of the hanging cords.

5 To make a counting code, take one doubled hanging cord and tie knots in it. A sample knot used in a *quipu* is shown here. Get creative and make up some of your own knots.

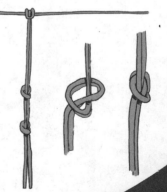

Chapter 9
North America

People began migrating from Europe and Asia to North America at least 12,000 years ago, and possibly as long as 60,000 years ago. As they spread out across the continent, they developed different cultures and lifestyles.

Many aspects of Native American mythology are shared throughout North America. But people in the Arctic **tundra**, the woodlands of the East, the deserts of the Southwest, and along the Pacific Coast also created their own stories, based on their particular surroundings.

There is still a lot about early Native American sacred traditions we don't know. They did not have writing to record their stories. Except for **adobe** and **cliff dwellings** in the Southwest, Native American buildings were mostly **longhouses** and other types of wooden structures that did not last. The only large monuments Native Americans left behind were rock paintings and carvings in the Southwest, and grassy ceremonial mounds in the Northeast and Midwest.

In North America, as in Central and South America, much native culture was lost or destroyed when European explorers and settlers took over. Native Americans did succeed in preserving some aspects of their heritage, though. In recent years, they have agreed to share some of these with the world, but have also chosen to keep many of their sacred traditions within their own community.

Did You Know?

Native Americans in the Pacific Northwest tell stories about the battles between Thunderbird and Whale. They caused the earth to shake and the waters to rise up. Today some scientists believe these stories can be linked to an actual earthquake and **tsunami** that hit the area in 1700 CE.

Words to Know

tundra: a treeless Arctic plain of moss and shrubs covering a layer of permanently frozen soil.

adobe: building material made of sun-dried mud and straw.

cliff dwelling: homes built on rock ledges or in cliffs by prehistoric Native Americans in the Southwest.

longhouse: a long arched Native American style of house big enough for several families. Built of logs and covered with bark and skins.

tsunami: an enormous wave caused by an underwater earthquake.

Native Americans lived in ways that were deeply connected with the earth. So it's not surprising that Native American mythology is filled with stories about spirits of plants, animals, the land, and the sky.

The most important plant to Native Americans was corn. Corn was first grown in Mexico and slowly spread throughout the rest of the continent. Native Americans figured out how to make corn produce bigger and tastier ears.

Then they figured out how to speed up its growing time so it could be planted farther north, where the summers were shorter. Throughout North America there are stories of corn goddesses and gods.

Native Americans everywhere also had stories of the Three Sisters—corn, squash, and beans. Planting these three vegetables together made for better gardens. Squash grows on a low-lying vine with big flat leaves that spread across the ground, keeping moisture in and weeds out. Beans fertilize the soil by taking nitrogen out of the air through its leaves and sending it out through its roots. They grow on climbing vines that wrap themselves around the tall stalks of corn for support. In the creation story of the Iroquois Confederacy in Upstate New York, Ataentsic the Sky Woman brings mankind the Three Sisters.

Sedna

The Inuit people of Alaska and Canada tell the story of Sedna, sea goddess of the chilly north. A bird convinced Sedna to run away from her father and marry him. But she grew unhappy, and begged her father to rescue her. The bird and his friends attacked Sedna and her father as they paddled away in his kayak. Sedna's father tried to throw her overboard to save himself, but she clung to the side of the kayak. He finally had to cut off her fingers, which turned into seals and whales. Sedna sank to the bottom of the ocean, where she ruled over all creatures. Inuit hunters make sure to honor Sedna so they will have a good catch. In 2004, Sedna gained new fame when a tiny frozen planetoid at the edge of the solar system was named after her.

An Iroquois Creation Story

Long ago, water covers the entire earth. Ataentsic, Sky Woman, lives with her husband, Sky Chief, in Karonhiake, or Sky World. Sky Woman is expecting a baby, and she asks her husband to make her some tea from the roots of the Tree of Life. But as he digs for the roots, the dirt caves in and the tree falls through towards Earth's waters.

As Sky Woman bends down to see the hole she falls in, grabbing some seeds from the Tree of Life as she falls. Some geese catch Sky Woman, but she is too heavy for them to carry back up to Sky World. They lower her onto the back of a great turtle floating on the water covering Earth.

Sky Woman thanks the creatures but tells them that she needs dirt to live on. So the muskrats and the otters dive down to the bottom of the water and bring back some grains of dirt. Sky Woman dances and sings in a circle, and both the turtle's shell and the dirt spread to form the land. Then she drops the seeds from the Tree of Life and plants grow up everywhere.

Sky Woman has a baby girl. When the girl grows up, she takes a walk to the west. The wind starts to blow and a cloud moves towards her. She faints, and when she awakens she finds two crossed arrows on her stomach. She is the bride of the Spirit of the West Wind, and will have twin boys.

The twins fight before they are even born. Hahgwehdiyu, the right-handed twin, is born the usual way. Hahgwehdaetgah, the left-handed twin, pushes his way out of his mother's armpit and kills her. They bury her, and from her head grow the Three Sisters—corn, beans, and squash. From her heart grows sacred tobacco, and from her feet wild strawberry, known as the Big Medicine. She is Mother Earth, because she supports the people, animals, and plants.

The twins grow up and create everything, including rivers, mountains, and human beings. But they still fight. Eventually Hahgwehdiyu whacks his brother with a big thorny stick and sends him to the underworld. Hahgwehdiyu becomes keeper of the day and Hahgwehdaetgah keeper of the night. When Sky Woman dies her head is flung into the night sky. She becomes Grandmother Moon. The humans are left to take care of the world and keep everything in balance.

Plant a Native American Three Sisters Garden

You can grow a Three Sisters Garden pretty much anywhere. Plant your seeds as early as possible in the spring, as soon as the weather has turned warm.

1 Make a mound of soil about 12 inches (30 centimeters) high. The top of the mound should be flat.

2 In the center of the mound, plant five or six corn kernels in a small circle. Water the seeds.

3 Wait a week or two until the corn is 6 inches (15 centimeters) high. Then plant seven or eight pole beans in a circle about 6 inches (15 centimeters) away from the corn.

4 Wait another week, then plant seven or eight squash seeds around the edge of the mound.

5 As the bean plants grow, you can help them wrap around the cornstalks.

6 Keep your garden weeded and watered. Your harvest should be ready in two or three months.

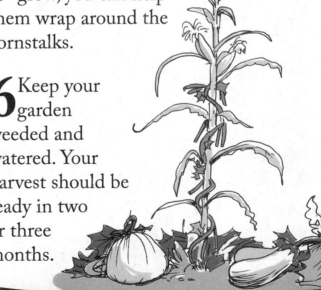

Make Native American Three Sisters Succotash

This Native American vegetable stew can be made with frozen vegetables or fresh vegetables from the market or your own Three Sisters Garden.

Supplies

- medium saucepan
- 1 cup (250 ml) water
- 1 small bag frozen lima beans
- 1 small bag frozen corn kernels
- 1 small bag frozen zucchini, sliced
- butter, salt, and pepper to taste

1 Pour the water into the saucepan and cover. Bring to a boil over medium heat.

2 Place vegetables in the saucepan and return to a boil.

3 Turn down the heat and let simmer (gently bubbling) for 10-15 minutes.

4 Serve with butter, salt, and pepper.

Did You Know?

One Native American tradition was to give a basket of corn kernels to a person who was listening to a long story. As each line was spoken, the person would take one kernel out of the basket. After the story was finished, the listener would slowly eat the corn to help him remember the story he had just heard.

Did You Know?

Many Native American stories feature animal tricksters like coyote, raven or crow, and rabbit who act like humans. They use their wits to get out of trouble or play jokes on others, but they can also represent creator spirits. In one story coyote was given the job of placing the stars in the sky. But he made a mess of it, and from then on, he howled whenever he looked at the night sky. Another well-known trickster is Kokopelli, a humpbacked flute player. Kokopelli may be based on the desert robber fly, which has a curved back and long, flute-like snout.

Hopi Mythology

To the Hopi people of the southwestern United States, **kachinas** are the spirits of their ancestors. They dwell in the mountain ranges of Arizona and return to their descendants in the form of rain that helps the crops grow.

There are hundreds of different kachinas, representing all aspects of life: plants, animals, the sun, and death. Some of the kachina spirits are clowns. Some are monsters who scare children into behaving properly. And some are messengers between humans and gods. Strange-looking mudheads are warriors and magician spirits. But the kachinas' most important job is making rain.

The oldest evidence of kachina culture found on pottery and rock art dates back about 700 years. Some were borrowed from the neighboring Zuni people. And some may trace their way back to much older civilizations in Mexico.

Today Hopis still hold ceremonies in which dancers dress up like kachinas and act out ancient rituals. In some the kachinas emerge from **kivas** to symbolize their birth into the world. In other ceremonies they interact with the entire community in the role of the spirit they represent.

Hopi children are taught to recognize all the different spirits with special kachina dolls. Before the ceremonial season begins, fathers and uncles carve and paint the miniature kachinas.

Words to Know

kachina: a Hopi ancestral spirit.
kiva: a round, underground ceremonial chamber.

The Kachinas and the Little Girl

The people in a Hopi village are afraid because the kachinas are stealing their children. One woman catches her little daughter following her as she goes out to get water. She is so upset that she throws a stone at the child and warns her to go back home. But the girl just sits down and begins to cry. A kachina feels sorry for the girl, and he picks her up and carries her to his village.

All the kachinas are happy to see the visitor, and serve her melons and peaches and corn. The child eats and eats until she is full. She's happy to stay with the kachinas, who dance at night and hold huge feasts. But soon she becomes homesick. She is so sad she does not eat or talk.

In her old village the little girl's parents are sick with worry because they miss their daughter. The kachinas tell the girl to prepare herself with a new dress and moccasins. They load up baskets with corn, beans, meat, and melons. And they set off for the village, singing and walking and bringing the rain with them. The girl runs into her house to wake her parents. Behind her come the kachinas with their baskets of food, which they give to the entire village. But when they leave, the rain goes with them.

Everyone is happy for a while. Eventually the people eat all the food the kachinas brought them and grow hungry. The little girl remembers life with the kachinas, and wishes she could go back. She becomes so sad that she falls ill. When she dies, she returns once again to the village of the kachinas.

During the ceremonies the dolls are presented to young girls. The children take them home and learn the markings and dress of each particular spirit.

Traditional kachina dolls are made from round columns of wood from dried cottonwood roots. They are decorated with painted-on clothes and abstract features. Sometimes they wear capes. Today some artists also make kachina dolls just for tourists. These collector items come with realistic fabric costumes and feathered headpieces.

Make a Hopi Kachina Doll

In this project, you'll create your own kachina doll, based on whatever is most important to you. Choose a theme for your kachina, then create a costume that goes along with it.

1 To indicate the kachina's head on the tube or dowel, draw a line around the body about one-third of the way down. Draw or paint on a face. Eyes can be shown as slits, stars, or almond-shaped. Some kachina faces have circles, squares, or upside-down Vs drawn around their nose and eyes.

2 Draw on arms or attach craft sticks or cardboard to make arms that stick out.

3 Make a headdress by taping feathers to the inside of the tube so they stick out the top. Or make a board for the back of the head from a decorated square of cardboard and glue it on.

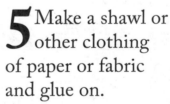

4 To make tassels, loop some string around your fingers a few times. Tie a short piece of string tightly around the top of the loop. Cut the bottom of the loop to make the strands. Glue on.

5 Make a shawl or other clothing of paper or fabric and glue on.

Important Names

Acheron: (Greek) son of Apollo/Helios.

Achilles: (Greek) hero of Trojan War.

Aeneas: (Roman) hero of *The Aeneid*.

Aido-Hwedo: (African) Rainbow Snake.

Allah: (Muslim) deity in the Koran.

Amaterasu: (Japanese) sun goddess.

Anansi: (Ashanti) trickster spider.

Anubis: (Egyptian) god of embalming.

Aphrodite: (Greek) goddess of love.

Apollo: (Greek)/Roman god of light, music, and medicine.

Arachne: (Greek) spinner turned into a spider by Athena.

Ares: (Greek) god of war.

Ariadne: (Greek) daughter of Minos who helped Theseus kill the Minotaur.

Artemis: (Greek) goddess of the hunt.

Arthur: (English) mythical hero king.

Asclepius: (Greek) god of medicine.

Asgard: (Norse) home of the gods.

Ataentsic: (Iroquois) Sky Woman creator.

Athena: (Greek) goddess of wisdom.

Babalu-Aye: (Yoruba) god of healing.

Bacchus: (Roman) god of wine.

Balder: (Norse) beloved son of Odin and Frigga.

Belenus: (Celtic) god of farming.

Beowulf: (English) epic hero.

Brahma: (Hindu) creator deity.

Brigid: (Irish) goddess of fire, connected with Christian Saint Brigid.

Buddha: (Buddhist) founder of Buddhism.

Camelot: (England) site of King Arthur's court.

Cerberus: (Greek) three-headed guard dog of underworld.

Ceres: (Roman) goddess of the harvest.

Charybdis: (Greek) sea nymph/whirlpool in *The Odyssey*.

Circe: (Greek) witch who captures Odysseus in *The Odyssey*.

Coatlcue: (Aztec) goddess of the earth.

Confucius: (China) philosopher founder of Confucianism.

Cronus: (Greek) ruler of the Titans, deity of time.

Cuchulainn: (Celtic) hero son of Lugh.

Cupid: (Roman) god of desire.

Cybele: (Roman) Great Mother goddess brought from Turkey.

Daedalus: (Greek) mythical inventor of the labyrinth.

Darama: (Australian) Great Spirit.

Demeter: (Greek) goddess of the harvest.

Deucalion and **Pyrrha:** (Greek) figures in flood story.

Devi: (Hindu) goddess, also known as the warlike Durga, Kali "the dark one," and Parvati, wife of Shiva.

Diana: (Roman) goddess of the hunt.

Dido: (Roman) queen of Carthage in *The Aeneid*.

Dionysos: (Greek) god of wine.

Eastre: (Anglo-Saxon) goddess of spring and rebirth.

Ector: (English) foster father of King Arthur.

Enki: (Mesopotamian) god of freshwater.

Enkidu: (Mesopotamian) wild man in epic of *Gilgamesh*.

Epimetheus: (Greek) brother of Prometheus, husband of Pandora.

Eros: (Greek) god of desire.

Eshu: messenger and trickster.

Faunus: (Roman) god of woods and fields.

Feng-po: (China) goddess of wind.

Fenrir: (Norse) wolf-son of Loki.

Finn MacCool: (Celtic) hero.

Frigga: (Norse) wife of Odin.

Fu Xi: (China) god of creativity.

Gaea: (Greek) deity of the earth.

Galahad: (English) hero of King Arthur legends.

Ganesha: (Hindu): god of good luck and wisdom.

Geb: (Egyptian) Earth god.

George Lucas: (American) creator of Star Wars.

Gilgamesh: (Mesopotamian) hero.

God: Jewish and Christian deity in the Bible.

Gong Gong: (China) god of water.

Grendel and **Grendel's mother:** (English) monsters from Beowulf.

Hades: (Greek) god of the underworld and name of the underworld.

❋ Important Names ❋

Hahgwehdaetgah: (Iroquois) keeper of the night.

Hahgwehdiyu: (Iroquois) keeper of the day.

Hanuman: (Hindu) monkey god.

Heimdall: (Norse) sentry god to Asgard.

Hel: (Norse) goddess of the underworld.

Helen of Troy: (Greek) mythical beauty who started the Trojan War.

Helios: (Greek) god of the sun.

Hephaestus: (Greek) god of fire.

Hera: (Greek) queen of the gods.

Heracles: (Greek) hero.

Hercules: (Roman) hero.

Hermes: (Greek) god of merchants and thieves.

Hesiod: (Greek) author of Theogon.

Hestia: (Greek) goddess of the hearth.

Hippolyte: (Greek) mythic queen of the Amazons.

Hoder: (Norse) blind brother of Balder.

Homer: (Greek) composer of *The Odyssey* and *The Iliad*.

Horus: (Egyptian) god of the sky.

Huitzilopochtli: (Aztec) "Hummingbird of the South," god of war and the sun.

Hun Hunahpu and **Vucub Hunahpu:** (Mayan) god of fertility and his brother.

Hunahpu and **Ixbalanque:** (Mayan) Hero Twins.

Hygeia: (Greek) goddess of health.

Icarus: (Greek) son of Daedalus who flew too near the sun.

Inti: (Incan): god of the sun.

Ishtar: (Mesopotamian) goddess of love.

Isis: (Egyptian) goddess of motherhood and family.

Izanagi: (Japanese) god of life.

Izanami: (Japanese) goddess of death.

Janus: (Roman) god of entryways.

Jesus Christ: (Christian) deity in New Testament of the Bible.

Joseph Campbell: (American) mythology scholar.

Juno: (Roman) queen of the gods.

Jupiter: (Roman) ruler of the gods.

Karonhiake: (Iroquois) Sky World.

Kay: (English) foster brother of King Arthur.

King Arthur and **the Knights of the Round Table:** (English) heroes.

Lao-Zi: (China) founder of Taoism.

Lif and **Lifthrasir:** (Norse) human survivors of end of the world.

Livinia: (Roman) wife of Aeneas in *The Aeneid*.

Loki: (Norse) shape-shifting trickster.

Lugh: (Celtic) god of light.

Manco Capoc: (Incan) Inti's son.

Mani: (Norse) moon god.

Manu: (Hindu) first man.

Mars: (Roman) god of war.

Mercury: (Roman) god of merchants and thieves.

Merlin: (English) magician tutor of King Arthur.

Metis: (Greek) mother of Athena.

Midgard: (Norse) home of humans.

Midgard Serpent: (Norse) monsterous snake that rings the human world.

Minerva: (Roman) goddess of wisdom.

Minos: (Greek) mythic king who kept the Minotaur in the labyrinth.

Minotaur: (Greek) half-man, half-bull monster.

Modi and Magni: (Norse) sons of Thor.

Mount Olympus: (Greek) home of the gods.

Nakawe: Mexican goddess of Earth.

Neptune: (Roman) god of the sea.

Nike: (Greek) goddess of victory.

Noah: Middle Eastern figure in Bible's flood story.

Nu-Gua: (China) goddess creator of humans.

Nut: (Egyptian) goddess of the sky.

Nyame: (Ashanti) supreme being.

Odin: (Norse) ruler of the gods (also known as Woden).

Odysseus: (Greek) hero of *The Odyssey*.

Olorun: (Yoruba) supreme being.

Onogoro: (Japan) first island.

Oonagh: (Celtic) wife of Finn MacCool.

Orpheus and **Eurydice:** (Greek) mythical singer and wife he tries to rescue from Hades.

Osiris: (Egyptian) god of the underworld.

Ovid: (Greek) composer of *Metamorphosis*.

Pan: (Greek) god of woods and fields.

Panacea: (Greek) goddess of healing potions.

Pandora: (Greek) mythic woman who released evil into the world.

Pan-gu: (China) primal giant.

Paris: (Greek) mythical prince who steals Helen of Troy.

Penelope: (Greek) Odysseus' wife in *The Odyssey*.

Persephone: (Greek) wife or Hades.

Pluto: (Roman) god of the underworld.

Polyphemus: (Greek) Cyclopes who captures Odysseus in *The Odyssey*.

Poseidon: (Greek) god of the sea.

Prometheus: (Greek) Titan who gave man fire.

Quetzalcoatl: (Aztec) "Feathered Serpent," god of wind.

Ra: (Egyptian) sun god.

Rainbow Serpent: (Australian) Dreamtime creator deity.

Rama: (Hindu) avatar of Vishnu, hero of Ramayana.

Ravana: (Hindu) demon king in Ramayana.

Rhea Silvia: (Roman) mother of Romulus and Remus in *The Aeneid*.

Rhea: (Greek) wife of Cronus, mother of Zeus.

River Styx: (Greek) river leading to Hades.

Romulus and **Remus:** (Roman) founders of Rome in *The Aeneid*.

Saturn: (Roman) ruler of the Titans, deity of time.

Scylla: (Greek) sea nymph/monster in *The Odyssey*.

Seth: (Egyptian) god of chaos.

Shango: god of thunder.

Shang-Ti: (China) ancient supreme being.

Shiva: (Hindu) destroyer deity.

Shu: (Egyptian) god of air.

Siddhartha Gautama: (Buddhist) Indian prince who became the Buddha.

Sita: (Hindu) wife of Rama, avatar of Lakshmi, goddess of wealth in Ramayana.

Skoll and Hati: (Norse) giant wolf brothers.

Snorri Sturluson: (Norse) author of *Prose Edda*.

Sol: (Norse) sun goddess.

Susanowo: (Japanese) god of storms.

Tefnut: (Egyptian) goddess of moisture.

Telemachus: (Greek) Odysseus' son in *The Odyssey*.

Tezcatlipoca: (Aztec) "Smoking Mirror," god of death and temptation.

Theseus: (Greek) hero who slew the Minotaur.

Thetis: (Greek) sea nymph and mother of Achilles.

Thomas Malory: (English) author of *Morte d'Arthur* about King Arthur.

Thor: (Norse) god of thunder.

Three Sisters: (North American) corn, squash, and beans.

Tian: (China) heaven.

Tlaloc: (Aztec) god of rain.

Tsuk-Yumi: (Japanese) god of the moon.

Tyr: (Norse) god of war.

Ulysses: (Roman) hero of *The Odyssey*.

Uranus: (Greek) deity of the sky.

Uther Pendragon: (English) father of King Arthur.

Utnapishtim: (Mesopotamian) flood story figure.

Uzume: (Japanese) goddess of dancing.

Valhalla: (Norse) drinking hall of heroes.

Venus: (Roman) goddess of love.

Vesta: (Roman) goddess of the hearth.

Victoria: (Roman) goddess of victory.

Vidar and Vali: (Norse) sons of Odin.

Viracocha: (Incan) creator god.

Virgil: (Roman) author of *The Aeniad*.

Vishnu: (Hindu) protector deity.

Vulcan: (Roman) god of fire.

Watakame: (Mexican) figure in flood story.

Xibalba: (Mayan) underworld.

Yggsdrasill: (Norse) gigantic tree connecting nine worlds in its roots and branches.

Yomi-tsu-kuni: (Japan) underworld.

Zeus: (Greek) ruler of the gods.

Zhu Rong: (China) god of fire.

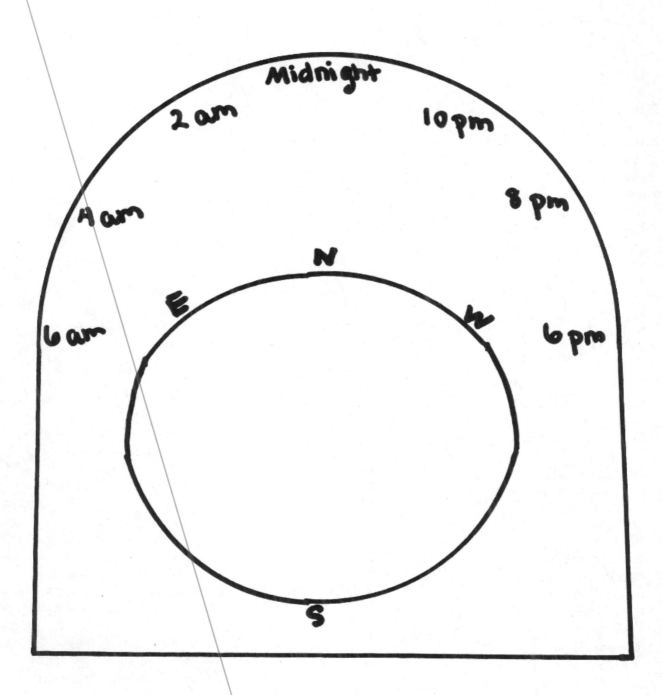

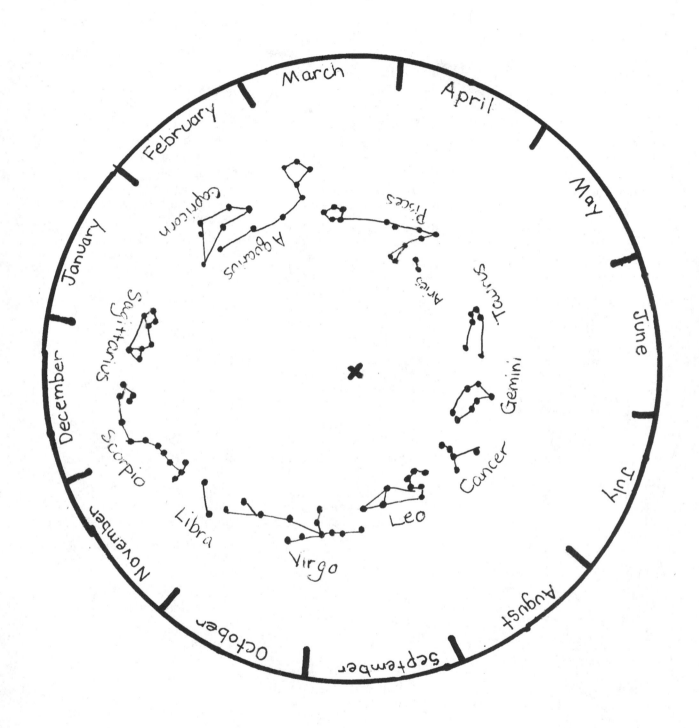

Glossary

Aborigine: original people living in Australia.

Adinkra: Ashanti symbols that represent proverbs.

adobe: a building material made of sun-dried mud and straw.

Achilles' heel: a person's weak spot.

allusion: an indirect reference to something from a story.

Amazon: a race of female warriors.

amulet: a charm to protect against evil.

ancestor: people who came before you, like your grandparents.

animist: a belief that objects and parts of nature have spirits.

anvil: a heavy iron block used with a hammer for shaping metal.

appease: to satisfy with sacrificial offerings.

archaeologist: a scientist who studies ancient people and their cultures.

ark: a boat built by Noah to save his family and animals from the flood.

artifact: an ancient, man-made object.

avatar: a human form taken by a Hindu deity.

Bible: holy book shared, in part, by Jews and Christians.

Brahman: the spiritual energy of the universe.

caduceus: a rod with two snakes twisted around it.

calabash gourd: a large, hard squash that is dried and used to make bottles.

canopic: a jar used to hold the organs of an ancient Egyptian mummy.

caste: a social class in Hindu society that once determined a person's job and position by birth.

catapult: an ancient military machine for hurling objects.

causeway: a raised path across water.

chaos: the disorganization before the universe was divided into its separate parts.

Christian: belonging to a religion based on Jesus Christ and the Old and New Testaments of the Bible.

circumambulation: to walk around smomething in a ritual.

clan: extended family group.

Classical Age: the period of great accomplishments in the Greek and Roman Empires.

cliff dwelling: homes built on rock ledges or in cliffs by prehistoric Native Americans in the Southwest.

codex: ancient sacred book.

compass: a tool for drawing circles that has two arms joined at the top by a hinge which can open and close.

Communist: a type of government that includes, among other things, banning religion.

Confucius: Chinese philosopher who founded Confucianism based on order.

conquistador: Spanish conqueror.

constellation: a group of stars that makes up a picture or shape.

covenant: a lasting agreement.

culture: the beliefs and way of life of a group of people.

cuneiform: wedge-shaped writing.

decipher: to figure out the meaning of something.

deity: a god or goddess.

democracy: a government where the people are represented.

dharma: a person's duty to follow divine law.

Diwali: Hindu festival of lights celebrating the new year.

divine: to be a god or relating to a god.

Dreaming or Dreamtime: the time of creation in the mythology of the Australian Aborigines.

Glossary

druid: ancient Celtic priest.

dynasty: a family that rules a country for a long time.

ecliptic: the path the sun, moon, and planets appear to take across the sky.

embalming: to treat a dead body so it won't decay.

emu: a bird similar to an ostrich but smaller.

epic poem: a long poem about the adventures of a hero told on a grand scale.

eternal: lasting forever.

fable: a story with a lesson.

fissure: crack in the ground.

forge: a furnace for melting metal to make tools and other objects.

fresco: a wall painting made in wet plaster.

furies: female monsters with leathery wings who seek revenge on mortals.

god: a superhuman or supernatural being who may have powers.

grid: a pattern of identical boxes.

hearth: fireplace for cooking in the home.

hero: a man, woman, or child who has the strength, wisdom, bravery, or beauty to do tasks that seem impossible.

hexagonal: having a shape with six straight, equal sides.

hieroglyphic: picture writing from ancient Egypt.

hilt: handle of a sword.

Hindu: main religion in India.

holy: sacred.

Holy Grail: the legendary cup used by Jesus at the Last Supper. Searched for by knights in medieval legends.

hunter-gatherers: people who get their food by hunting, fishing, and gethering wild plants instead of farming.

Hydra: a many-headed monster.

Ice Age: time when glaciers spread over large parts of the earth ending around 10,000 years ago.

immortality: being able to live forever.

initiation: a ceremony where a member of a group is given special privileges.

inundation: a flood.

irrigation: bringing water to the land to grow crops.

jaguar: a large wild cat from Central and South America with yellow fur and black spots.

Jewish: belonging to the religion based on God in the Old Testament of the Bible.

joust: a competition using weapons on horseback.

kachina: a Hopi ancestral spirit.

kami: Shinto nature gods.

karma: the actions that decide a person's next incarnation.

kiva: a round, underground ceremonial chamber

Koran: the Muslim sacred book.

labyrinth: a maze.

lair: hiding place.

lance: a sharp spear used by knights on horseback.

Last Supper: in the Bible, the last meal Jesus eats.

legend: a story about national heroes.

leprechaun: a little magical person from Irish mythology.

lever: a rod used for lifting things.

linen: cloth made from fiber of the flax plant.

literature: the written stories and history of a culture, language, or group of people.

llama: a member of the camel family from the Andes with a long neck, long fur, and small head. Used for wool and to carry supplies.

longhouse: a long arched Native American style of house big enough for several families. Built of logs and covered with bark and skins.

Glossary

lyre: a type of small harp.

Middle Ages: a period of time in Europe from the 400s to the 1400s CE.

minstrel: a performer who tells stories through song.

molten: melted.

missionary: someone sent to another country to spread their religion to the people there.

monotheistic: the belief in only one god.

monument: a site or structure that has special meaning.

moral: a lesson about the right way to behave.

mortal: an ordinary human, someone who does not live forever.

mosaic: a picture or design made from tiny tiles or stones.

myth: a story about gods or supernatural creatures that people once believed was true.

mythologist: someone who studies myths.

mythology: a collection of related myths from one culture.

natron: a natural salt used in embalming corpses.

nirvana: the state of bliss that is the goal of Buddhism.

Norse: people from Denmark, Norway, and Sweden.

Northern Hemisphere: the half of the earth north of the equator.

odyssey: a wandering adventure.

Old English: an early version of English used until about 1150 CE.

oracle: someone who makes mysterious prophecies.

oral tradition: a way of passing along important knowledge through storytelling or song instead of writing.

origin myth: creation myth.

page: a boy working as a knight's assistant.

panacea: something that is supposed to cure everything.

pantheon: all the gods from one tradition.

pastoral: relating to the countryside or rural life.

patron: supporter.

personification: a god or being that represents a thing or idea.

pestle: a club-shaped stick for crushing food or medicine.

pharaoh: ruler of ancient Egypt.

philosopher: someone who tries to understand and explain existence and reality.

philosophy: a way of thinking or set of beliefs.

pictographic: using pictures instead of letters to write.

plantain: a type of banana tree with long flat leaves.

primeval: from the beginning of time.

prophecy: being able to tell the future.

prosperity: wealth.

proverb: advice in the form of a well-known saying.

pyre: an outdoor fire used for burning a dead body in a funeral ceremony.

qi: the life-force inside everything.

quest: an adventurous journey in search of a specific goal.

quetzal: a Central American bird with green and red feathers and a long tail.

quipu: an Incan device made of string for keeping records.

rangoli: a geometric design drawn on the ground in front of a house.

rational thinking: thinking based on facts or reasons more than opinion or emotion.

Glossary

reed: a plant with a straight, tall stalk that grows in or near water.

reincarnation: rebirth in a new body or form of life.

relic: a sacred object connected with a holy person.

religion: a set of beliefs about reality and a god or gods.

resin: a sticky fluid made from plants that dries into a hard coating.

righteous: free from sin.

rune: mysterious Viking symbols.

rural: in the country, outside the city

sacred: extremely valuable to a culture, religion, or god.

sacrifice: killing a person or other living thing as an offering to a god or supernatural creature.

Santeria: a religion that combines Yoruba gods and Roman Catholic saints, said to involve animal sacrifice.

scholar: an expert who studies a subject.

shrine: a special place of worship.

sickle: a cutting tool with a curved blade.

siege: blocking off a city with an army to force it to surrender.

siren song: a call that tempts you to your doom.

slag: ash left from burning metal.

sling: a weapon with a strap for throwing small objects.

Southern Hemisphere: the half of the earth south of the equator.

Spanish Inquisition: a court where people were put on trial for breaking church law.

spirit: a supernatural being.

spiritual: relating to religion or sacred things.

steam engine: a machine powered by boiling water.

strait: a narrow passage in a body of water.

stupa: a dome-shaped Buddhist shrine.

stylus: a pointed instrument used for writing.

Sub-Saharan: the part of Africa that lies south of the Sahara Desert.

supernatural or **superhuman:** outside the usual laws of nature, such as magic.

Taoism: a Chinese religion and philosophy based on accepting the world.

Theogony: an account of the beginnings and family connections of the gods.

Titans: in Greek mythology, a race of giant deities who rule the earth before the gods.

tlachtli: Mayan ball court.

tournament: a series of knightly jousts and other competitions.

trickster: a person, animal, or god who tries to outsmart other characters for fun, greed, or revenge.

Trimurti: the three main gods in Hinduism.

tsunami: an enormous wave caused by an underwater earthquake.

tundra: a treeless Arctic plain of moss and shrubs covering a layer of permanently frozen soil.

unity: many things made into one.

Voodoo: a religion based on Yoruba gods said to involve witchcraft.

vulnerable: unprotected.

whirlpool: a spinning funnel of water that can pull things down.

yam: an edible root similar to a sweet potato.

yang: the light, active male spirit.

yin: the dark, passive female spirit.

ziggurat: ancient Mesopotamian temple shaped like a stepped pyramid with a shrine on top.

zodiac: the 12 constellations or "signs" located in the strip of sky that contains the paths of the sun, moon, and planets.

Resources

Books About Mythology

Davis, Kenneth C. *Don't Know Much About Mythology: Everything You Need to Know About the Greatest Stories in Human History But Never Learned.* HarperCollins, 2005.

Davis, Kenneth C. *Don't Know Much About World Myths.* HarperCollins Children's Books, 2005.

January, Brendan. *The New York Public Library Amazing Mythology: A Book of Answers for Kids.* John Wiley and Sons, 2000.

Mass, Wendy. *Gods and Goddesses.* Lucent Books, 2002.

Muten, Burleigh. *Goddesses: A World of Myth and Magic.* Barefoot Books, 2003.

Philip, Neil. *The Kingfisher Book of Mythology: Gods, Goddesses, and Heroes from Around the World.* Kingfisher Publications, 2001.

Philip, Neil. *Mythology.* Dorling Kindersley, 2000.

Philip, Neil. *Mythology of the World.* Kingfisher Publications, 2004.

Willis, Roy (editor). *World Mythology.* Duncan Baird Publishers, 1993.

Collections of World Myths

Bell-Rehwoldt, Sheri. *Amazing Maya Projects You Can Build Yourself.* Nomad Press, 2006.

Bini, Renata. *A World Treasury of Myths, Legends, and Folktales: Stories From Six Continents.* Harry N. Abrams, 2000.

Bordessa, Kris. *Tools of the Ancient Greeks.* Nomad Press, 2006.

Dickinson, Rachel. *Tools of the Ancient Romans.* Nomad Press, 2006.

Hamilton, Edith. *Mythology: Timeless Tales of Gods and Heroes.* Grand Central Publishing, 1999

McCaughrean, Geraldine. *The Bronze Cauldron: Myths and Legends of the World.* Margaret K. McElderry, 1998.

McCaughrean, Geraldine. *The Crystal Pool: Myth and Legends of the World.* Margaret K. McElderry, 1999.

McCaughrean, Geraldine. *The Golden Hoard: Myths and Legends of the World.* Margaret K. McElderry, 1996.

McCaughrean, Geraldine. *The Silver Treasure: Myths and Legends of the World.* Margaret K. McElderry, 1997.

Mutén, Burleigh. *Goddesses: A World of Myth and Magic.* Barefoot Books, 2003.

Philip, Neil. *The Illustrated Book of Myths: Tales & Legends of the World.* Dorling Kindersley, 1995.

Randall, Ronne. *The Children's Book of Myths and Legends: Extraordinary Stories from Around the World.* Bookmart Ltd., 2001.

Van Vleet, Carmella, *Great Ancient Egypt Projects You Can Build Yourself.* Nomad Press, 2006.

Web Sites

The Big Myth Myths told with Flash animation and background information.
www.mythicjourneys.org/bigmyth/2_eng_myths.htm

Center for Story and Symbol
www.folkstory.com

Encyclopedia Mythica
www.pantheon.org

Godchecker A light-hearted catalog of gods from around the world. *www.godchecker.com*

History for Kids Information about ancient history, geography, science, and culture.
www.historyforkids.org

Mr. Donn's Ancient History Page Information for students about ancient history, including myths.
www.mrdonn.org/ancienthistory.html

Mythography *www.loggia.com/myth*

Mythweb Simple versions of Greek myths, with fun animated illustrations. *www.mythweb.com*

Sacred Texts *www.sacred-texts.com*

Scholastic Myths, Folktales and Fairytales Short versions of world myths, and "myth brainstorming machine."
http://teacher.scholastic.com/writewit/mff/index.htm

Windows to the Universe Mythology Myths related to astronomy.
www.windows.ucar.edu/cgi-bin/tour_def/mythology/mythology.html

Index

A

Aborigines, 12, 77, 81–84
Achilles, 37–39
activities (Make a...)
    Ashanti Adinkra Cloth, 63
    Babylonian Zodiac StarFinder,
      18–19
    Bata Thunder Drum, 60
    Beltane Flower Hair Wreath,
      52
    British Sword in the Stone, 54
    Buddhist Stone Stupa, 71
    Celtic Triskeles Armband, 53
    Chinese Wind Goddess Tiger
      Kite, 76
    Cuneiform Clay Tablet, 17
    Day of the Dead Calavera, 93
    Egyptian Mummy, 23
    Hopi Kachina Doll, 106
    Incan Quipu, 97
    Indoor Boomerang, 84
    Japanese Daruma Egg Doll,
      80
    Magic Square, 75
    Maya Ball Game, 89
    Mythic Allusions Collage, 27
    Native American Three Sisters
      Garden, 102
    Native American Three Sisters
      Succotash, 103
    Odyssey Whirlpool, 40
    Rainbow Myth Window
      Hanging, 12–13
    Rangoli Design, 68
    Runic Stones and Pouch, 55
    Triangle with a Compass and
      Ruler, 35
Adinkra cloth, 61–63
Aeneas, 41–42
Aeneid, The, 37, 41–42
Africa, 12, 56–63. *See also* Egypt
Amaterasu, 79
Anansi, 61, 62
Aphrodite, 37
Apollo, 33, 34
Arthur, King, 6, 46–48

Ashanti myths, 61–63
Athena, 30–31, 32, 37, 39
Australia, 12, 77–78, 81–84
Aztec civilization/myths, 86,
    90–93

B

Bata drum, 58–59
Beowulf, 6, 7, 48–49
Book of the Dead, 22
Brahma, 64–65
Buddhism/Buddhist myths,
    8, 69–71, 73, 78, 80

C

Celtic myths, 43, 44–46
Central and South America,
    85–97
China, 8, 69–76
Christianity/Christian myths,
    8–9, 10, 12, 24, 29, 86, 87
Coatlcue, 90
Codex/Codices, 87
Confucius/Confucianism, 72–73
creation myths, 4, 21, 24, 28–29,
    30, 50, 65, 74, 79, 83, 87, 91,
    95, 100–101
Cronus, 29
cuneiform, 15, 17
Cybele, 41

D

Daedalus, 32–33
day/month names,
    1, 41, 50
death/afterlife
    myths, 4, 5, 20,
    22, 23, 50, 65, 69,
    73, 105
Delphi oracle, 34
Devi, 66
Dreamtime, 81–83

E

Egypt, 4–5, 7, 20–23
end of the world myths, 4, 50–51
Eshu, 57
Euclid, 31, 35

F

Finn MacCool, 45
flood myths, 9, 10–12, 16
Fu-Xi, 74, 75

G

Ganesha, 66
Geb, 4, 21
Giant's Causeway, 45–46
Gilgamesh, 10, 15–16
gods/supernatural beings, 3, 4–7,
    10–12, 15–16, 20–22, 24, 26,
    28–34, 36–42, 43–45, 49–51,
    54, 56–58, 61–62, 64–76,
    78–79, 88, 90–92, 94–96,
    99–101, 104–105
Golden Swan, The, 70
Greece/Rome, 6–7, 8, 10, 12,
    25–42

Index

H

Helen of Troy, 36, 37
Hephaestus, 30
Hera, 28, 30, 37
Heracles/Hercules, 31, 32
Hermes, 33
heroes/hero tales, 3, 4, 6, 66–67, 86, 87, 88
Hinduism/Hindu myths, 11, 64–68
Hippocrates, 33
holidays, 6–7, 41, 45, 52, 68, 93
Homer, 6, 36–37
Hopi myths, 104–106
Horus, 20, 21
Huitzilopochtli, 90–91, 92
human sacrifices, 32, 44, 87, 88, 92
Hunahpu, 88

I

Icarus, 32–33
Iliad, The, 6, 36, 37–38
Inca civilization/myths, 86, 94–97
India, 8, 11, 64–71
Ishtar, 15–16
Isis, 21
Islamic myths, 24
Ixbalanque, 88
Izanami and Izanagi, 79

J

Japan, 5, 8, 12, 77–80
Judaism/Jewish myths, 10, 24

K

kachinas/kachina dolls, 104–106
King Arthur and Knights of the Round Table, 6, 46–48

L

Loki, 50, 51

M

Mahabharata, 66
Manco Capoc, 94, 95, 96
Manu, 11
map, vi–vii
Maya civilization/myths, 86–89
Mesopotamia, 10, 15–16
Mexico, 85–93
Middle East, 4–5, 7, 10, 14–24
Minotaur, 8, 32
Mount Olympus, 29, 30, 31, 32
mummies, 23, 44, 96
myths and legends
    African, 12, 56–63 (*See also* Egypt)
    Australian, 12, 77–78, 81–84
    Central/South American, 85–97

Chinese, 8, 69–76
creation myths, 4, 21, 24, 28–29, 30, 50, 65, 74, 79, 83, 87, 91, 95, 100–101
death/afterlife myths, 4, 5, 20, 22, 23, 50, 65, 69, 73, 105
definition of, 3
disappearance of, 9
end of the world myths, 4, 50–51
flood myths, 9, 10–12, 16
Greek/Roman, 6–7, 8, 10, 12, 25–42
hero tales, 3–4, 6, 66–67, 86–88
history of, 1–2, 4–6
Indian, 8, 11, 64–71
Japanese, 5, 8, 12, 77–80
Middle Eastern, 4–5, 7, 10, 14–24
nature myths, 4–5, 9, 78
North American, 11, 98–106 (*See also* Mexico)
northern European, 6, 12, 43–55
preservation of, 6–7
religious, 3, 8, 9, 10–12, 24, 29, 64–71, 73 (*See also* gods/supernatural beings; specific religions)
spread/change of, 8–9
trickster tales, 4, 50–51, 61, 104
types of myths, 4

N

Native Americans, 98–106
nature myths, 4–5, 9, 78
Noah, 10
Norse myths, 12, 43, 49–51, 54
North America, 11, 98–106. *See also* Mexico
northern Europe, 6, 12, 43–55
Nu-Gua, 74
Nut, 4–5, 21
Nyame, 61, 62

Index

O

Odin, 50, 51
Odyssey, The, 6, 36, 38–40
Olorun, 57
Orishas, 57–58
Osiris, 20, 21, 22

P

Pachacuti, 94–96
Pandora, 27
Paris, 37
Popul Vuh, 86–87, 88, 89
Prometheus, 32

Q

Quetzalcoatl, 91–92

R

Ra, 5, 21
Ragnarok, 50–51
Rainbow Serpent, 12, 83
Rama/Ramayana, 66–67
reincarnation, 65, 69, 73
religions, 3, 8, 9, 10–12, 24, 29, 48, 64–71, 73, 78, 80, 86, 87. *See also* gods/supernatural beings
Remus, 42
Rome/Greece, 6–7, 8, 10, 12, 25–42
Romulus, 42
runes, 55

S

Sedna, 100
Seth, 21
Shango/*Storm of Shango*, 57–58, 59
Shang-Ti, 72
Shinto, 78
Shiva, 64–65
Shu, 4, 21

Sirens, 38, 39
Sky Woman, 100–101
South and Central America, 85–97
stars/constellations, 16, 18–19, 82, 1, 92, 95, 104
sun/sun gods/goddesses, 4–5, 18, 21, 33, 39, 50, 51, 65, 72, 78, 79, 88, 91, 92, 94–96, 104

T

Taoism, 73
Tezcatlipoca, 91–92
Thor, 49, 51
Three Sisters, 100–101
Tian, 72, 73
timeline, iv–v
Tlaloc, 90, 91, 92
tricksters/trickster tales, 4, 50–51, 61, 104
Trojan War, 28, 36–40, 41–42
twins, 42, 57, 86, 87, 88, 101

U

Uluru (Ayer's Rock), 81

V

Vedas, 65
Viking/Norse myths, 12, 43, 48–51, 54
Viracocha, 95, 96
Virgil, 37, 41
Vishnu, 64–65, 66

W

Watakame, 11
writing, 7, 14, 15, 17, 22, 43, 44, 54, 61, 85, 87, 97

Y

Yoruba myths, 57–60

Z

Zeus, 10, 28, 29, 30, 32, 37, 40